Russia in Central Asia

MICHAEL RYWKIN

RUSSIA IN

CENTRAL ASIA

COLLIER BOOKS, New York
COLLIER-MACMILLAN LTD., London

A Collier Books Original

First Edition 1963

Collier Books is a division of
The Crowell-Collier Publishing Company

Library of Congress Catalog Card Number: 63-8136

Editor's Preface

THE REMARKABLE change in Russia's international position since the Second World War has brought forth an unprecedented demand for information about all aspects of the land of the Soviets. The press, radio, and television deal with current developments, but by their very nature they can provide only casual glimpses of the factors essential to an understanding of Soviet policies and of the peculiar twists of Russian events. Russia, moreover, is a vast, ancient, and fascinating country, and although her cultural achievements do not go much farther back than to the end of the eighteenth or the beginning of the nineteenth centuries, there is much about Russia that an informed person might like to know even if the Soviets had not arrived at their present sinister prominence.

Countless elements shape the life and policies of a nation, and the more we know about Russia's past and present, the better are our chances to comprehend her correctly. It is a notable and regrettable fact that until quite recently Russian studies were largely neglected in the West. A generation ago, interest in Russia was limited to a relatively small group of specialists and intellectuals; today there is a widespread and mounting demand for authoritative, dependable, and clearly presented information on tsarist Russia and the USSR. There are numerous books in English, some of them excellent, on the various aspects of the Russian scene, but other aspects have been left unexplored or call for fresh consideration.

The Russian Civilization Series of Collier Books, which deals with both the pre-revolutionary and the Soviet periods, is designed to meet, in part, this need. Each volume is written especially for Collier Books by a specialist in his field. The studies endeavor to maintain high levels of scholarship without being too technical and to present the information in an attractive and readable style. Each volume is complete in itself and can be used independently of the others in the series. Original works of distinction, which might formerly have been accessible to only a few, are now available to anyone who wishes to own them: the modest price of these books brings them within the reach of a wide public—with no sacrifice of scientific or literary standards.

Russian Central Asia, the vast subcontinent under Soviet rule, has attracted considerable attention in recent years, especially in connection with Moscow's huge program of industrialization and development of virgin land in that remote region. The success or failure of these plans is likely to exercise profound influence on the leadership of the Communist Party of the Soviet Union, the economic progress of the USSR, and the policies of Moscow both in Asia and in the West. Literature in English on the republics that form Russia's Central Asia is small and seldom deals with recent developments. It is hoped that the present volume will help to fill this gap.

Dr. Michael Rywkin, Assistant Professor at The City College of New York and, in 1962–1963, research fellow, Russian Research Center, Harvard University, spent four years in Central Asia and belongs to the small group of social scientists in this country who have good firsthand knowledge of that region. His book presents a brief outline of the eastward expansion of imperial Russia, but deals chiefly with the Soviet period and offers a penetrating analysis of the administrative, social, economic, and cultural policies of the Soviet Union in that part of the world. Under Soviet constitutional arrangements the Russian territories in Asia are sovereign republics, since colonialism, of course, is repugnant to Soviet political theory. In practice, however, the Central Asian republics are effectively controlled by the Kremlin. Dr. Rywkin gives a revealing account of the methods which allow the Communist Party of the Soviet Union and the Moscow government to combine total centralized control with the fiction of local sovereignty. The story he tells goes beyond the boundaries suggested by the title of his book and is actually a thorough exposition of Communist methods and policies in the underdeveloped countries.

MICHAEL T. FLORINSKY
General Editor
Russian Civilization Series

Columbia University, New York

Contents

Tables

Maps and Graphs

Russia in Central Asia

Chapter 1

Historical Background

The First Three Hundred Years
(From the 1550's to the 1850's)

RUSSIAN ATTEMPTS to establish relations with Central Asia can be traced back as far as the sixteenth century. The first Muscovite agent to penetrate the area (1558–1559) was an English merchant, Jenkinson, in the service of Tsar Ivan the Terrible. After 1565 several Russian missions went to Bukhara, Khiva and Samarkand. Simultaneously the Russians began their penetration of the immense and sparsely populated Siberia. The interregnum of the Time of Troubles (1605–1613) did not slow Russian movements eastward to Siberia, but neither was it conducive to new diplomatic openings in Central Asia. Order being re-established in Moscow, an envoy of the Emir of Bukhara arrived in 1619 to seek contacts with the first tsar of the new dynasty, Michael Fedorovich Romanov. To reciprocate, a Russian envoy, Ivan Khokhlov, was sent to Bukhara in 1621.

Mutual interest was, however, too limited and the travel too difficult to warrant any steady relations, and contacts between Moscow and Central Asia remained sporadic. After the Russians had reached the Pacific Ocean in their eastward penetration of Siberia, a *boyar* (aristocrat) from the Russian Caspian Sea harbor of Astrakhan, Ivan Fedotov, was sent to Khiva (1669), and the brothers Pazukhin to Bukhara and Balk (Balsh). In 1675 another Russian emissary, Vasily Daudov, and his party reached Bukhara.

With Peter the Great on the throne and the following westernization of Russia, superficial as it was, Russian interest in Central Asia increased. The new tsar was influenced by his natural curiosity, his passion to establish commercial relations with every possible country, even by his knowledge of colonial exploits of West European nations. He therefore wanted a more active policy in regard to Central Asia. In the meantime, in 1695 a Russian merchant by the name of Semen Malenkii reached India by way of Central Asia, but died on his return trip, unable to match the feat of his seafaring predecessor, Afanasii Nikitin (1469). The year 1700 brought two new developments which further increased Peter's interest in Central Asia. The first was a rumor about gold deposits in Central Asia, in the Amu-Darya area, and the second, an odd request for Russian protection by the Shah Niaz of Khiva, who was then involved in one of those endless feudal wars that usually plagued the area. At war with Sweden and Turkey, Peter had to postpone any positive action. But in 1715 he sent an expedition to the Kazakh Steppe, along the Irtysh and Erket rivers, and in 1716 a few forts were built on the Irtysh. Finally, in 1717 an expedition under the command of Prince A. Bekovich-Cherkassky went to Khiva. This expedition, 6,655 men strong, was equipped at a cost of a quarter of a million rubles. They were instructed to study the flow of Amu-Darya, to reroute the river, if possible, to flow back to the Caspian Sea and to build a fort on the Amu-Darya shores. In addition to that, Bekovich-Cherkassky was to induce the rulers of Khiva and Bukhara to accept nomad Kazakhs, friendly to Russia, into their personal guards. The Khivans, who never considered their former offer too seriously, as it was made amidst internal struggles, showed little enthusiasm for the Russians. Under the pretext of providing adequate living quarters, the Russians were split into small units and massacred. Most of those who escaped perished in the desert, and only a few found their way back home. All that was left was a small fort on the eastern shore of the Caspian Sea, which was abandoned two years later. The tragic end of the Khivan venture did not discourage the tsar; in 1718 his envoy, Florio Beneveni, arrived in Bukhara and stayed there until the Emperor's death in 1725.

With the death of Peter the Great and the consequent evacuation of the Persian Caspian Sea shore by Russian troops (1732), Russia temporarily discontinued all attempts to penetrate Central Asia, concentrating her efforts on extending her influence in the Kazakh Steppe, an enormous, sparsely inhabited area located between Siberia and Central Asia proper. The 1731 acceptance by the Kazakhs of the Lesser Horde, wandering in the steppes southeast of the Ural river, of nominal Russian sovereignty, was the first step in that direction. A series of forts were built on the Ural river in 1735, facing the newly acquired but unruly "vassals." Russian Cossacks settled around these forts and around the previously built Irtysh forts. The first have since been known as Ural and Orenburg Cossacks, the latter as Siberian Cossacks. The Kazakhs of the Lesser Horde, separated by fortifications from Russian territory, maintained their old way of life. The Middle Horde accepted Russian sovereignty in 1740 and then changed in favor of Chinese sovereignty in 1742, but soon thereafter renounced both. From then on, for three-quarters of a century, the political picture of the area remained static. Russia was unwilling at that time to undertake any new ventures in the steppes and deserts of Kazakhstan. The Kazakhs in the steppe and the Cossacks around the forts maintained an uneasy truce with the Russian garrisons in the forts who were to protect peace and order. The Kazakhs were more disturbed by the unfriendly Cossack attitude than by nominal Russian sovereignty, which even the Middle Horde came gradually to accept. The first important Russian intervention in Kazakh affairs occurred at the turn of the century when Emperor Paul I approved the break-off of the Western part of the Lesser Horde from the main body. The new group became known as the Bukeev Horde. At the same time, in accordance with his new alliance with Napoleon, Paul I organized an expedition of 22,500 Don Cossacks, under General Vasily Orlov, to Orenburg with the mission to proceed through Bukhara and Khiva to India. Although the main goal of the expedition was to attack the British in India, instructions were given to Orlov to take possession of Bukhara and to liberate Russian slaves in Khiva. This plan was not new; in 1791 Catherine the Great toyed with a similar plan. The assassination of Paul and the reversal of Russian foreign policy stopped the expedition.

Following the victory over Napoleon and Russia's emergence as a great power in Europe, a radical change in Russian policy occurred toward the Kazakh Steppe. The Emperor Alexander I decided to transform Russia's relationships with the Lesser and Middle Hordes. A special Kazakh code was drafted in 1822 by his otherwise liberal advisor, Speransky. The khanate of the Middle Horde was abolished, and its territory, inhabited by about a half million people, was divided into Russian administrative units with mixed administration. Russian military jurisdiction was established over all criminal offenses as well as over all civil litigations involving over twenty rubles. Acquisition of new slaves among Kazakhs was prohibited. Russian sovereignty over the area ceased to be nominal and became a reality. Two years later (1824) the half million nomads of the Lesser Horde were affected by similar reforms, but local administration was left in the hands of three native "sultans," each to be responsible for a part of the territory. Simultaneously, Cossacks were permitted to use "hot pursuit" in following unruly Kazakh bands into their own territory. Kazakh pasture lands near Russian fortifications were expropriated and given to the Cossacks.

Such an abrupt end of Kazakh independence led to numerous revolts. Kaip Gallia Ishimov, son of a former khan of the Lesser Horde, rose against the Russians in 1818–20 and again in 1827–29, trying to re-establish the khanate by accepting the sovereignty of the Central Asian Khan of Kokand. Isatai and Makambat led revolts in the Bukeev Horde in 1836–38, and Sardzhan in the Middle Horde in 1832–36. At the same time (1834) Russian Orenburg authorities built the Novo-Aleksandrovsk fort on the eastern shore of the Caspian on the spot which had been abandoned since the days of Bekovich-Cherkassky.[1]

In order to "encourage trade" between the Cossacks, engaged in agriculture, and the Kazakhs, traditionally nomad cattle breeders, the latter were forbidden to cultivate their land. This discriminatory policy forced the Kazakhs to buy Russian bread at high prices and to sell their cattle at low prices, and was enforced during the 1830's.

In 1837 the Russian government, in order to improve the collection of taxes from the Kazakhs of the Lesser Horde, established a hut tax of 1.50 rubles, and the old method of collecting taxes through the intermediary of Kazakh authorities was discarded.

Dissatisfaction with Russian policies brought about a large-scale revolt in 1838 in western and northern Kazakhstan, which was especially fierce in the Akmolinsk area. The Kazakhs, led by an energetic leader, Kenesary, kept the area in turmoil until 1845. Kenesary wanted to return to the pre-1822 relations, that is, to a purely nominal Russian sovereignty. Unable to force Russian consent, Kenesary sought cooperation from the three khans of Turkestan and tried to destroy Russian forts and Cossack settlements.

Finally defeated, he moved south into the territory of the Greater Horde, which was still outside Russian control, where he perished in a local clash.

In the meantime Russia continued to attempt to establish diplomatic and commercial relations with the states of Kokand, Bukhara and Khiva, south of the Kazakh Steppe. In 1803 an armed caravan under Lieutenant Gaverdovsky tried to reach Bukhara from Siberia, but, on encountering Kazakh hostility, turned back.

In 1820 a foreigner in the Russian service, Negri, reached Bukhara and managed to collect useful information. A new caravan, sent in 1824 in an attempt to foster commercial relations, lost all its merchandise.

In 1833 a very energetic general, V. A. Perovsky, became governor of Orenburg, and a more active policy was started toward Central Asia. In 1835 Vitkevich, a Polish officer who took part in the Polish revolt of 1830 and was subsequently exiled to Siberia, was sent by the Russian government to Central Asia. Vitkevich, hoping to gain amnesty, was very enterprising. He reached Bukhara and from there went to Afghanistan, staying from 1837 to 1839 and successfully counteracting the intrigues of a British agent named Burns, who was the first Westerner since Marco Polo to reach the mountains of Pamir. In 1839 an armed conflict broke out between Britain and Afghanistan. British troops took Kandahor and Kabul. Russia was far from pleased, and felt justified compensating herself. General Perovsky was given orders to move on Khiva, to replace the Khan with a more compliant one, to obtain trade privileges and to free Russian prisoners. The six-thousand-man expeditionary force included one hundred fifty Bashkir and one thousand Kazakh auxiliary troops with twelve thousand camels. Perovsky failed, however, to reach Khiva and, after losing in the desert over a thousand men and almost all the camels, turned back, lucky to avoid the fate of his predecessor of 120 years before, Bekovich-Cherkassky.

The British were no more successful in Afghanistan. Initial victories were followed by defeat in 1841. Although both Russia and Britain had a difficult start, neither gave up. Britain continued its penetration of Afghanistan, and new Russian missions went to Bukhara (Major Butenev) and Khiva (Captain Nikiforov). A group of Russian merchants, eager to imitate the highly successful British East India Company, organized the "Moscow Trading House for Commerce with Asia" in 1847. The tsarist government, unaccustomed to private ventures of such a scale, was unwilling to back the colonization plans of the new company, and the latter was closed in 1854, having accomplished nothing.

By 1817, two years after the Kenesary revolt, the Russians felt secure enough to make a major move toward Central Asia. The local Russian commander, General Obruchev, constructed Fort Raim (Aralskoe) on the northern shore of Syr-Darya. Two vessels were brought by land to the Aral Sea and reassembled there. The fort became the main base for further Russian penetration into Central Asia. In the years following, several new forts were built on the banks of the Syr-Darya river, bringing Russia five hundred miles closer to the khanates of Turkestan by eliminating the protective no man's land of the "hungry steppes" between the Ural and Syr-Darya rivers. The line of forts was completed in 1853 with the seizure of Ak Mechet (Perovsk) from Kokand in reprisal for a raid of nomad Kokand Kazakhs on the Russian Fort Raim.

The other arm of the huge Russian pioneer movement was moving south from Siberia along Chinese borders, through the lands of the Middle Horde and across the lake of Balkhash. By so doing, the Russians succeeded in forcing the Kazakhs of the Greater Horde to shift their allegiance from Kokand to Russia (1847). Pushing further south, they erected Fort Vernoe (now Alma-Ata, the capital of Kazakhstan). This was the first of a new line of forts that the Russians constructed to seal the northern borders of Kokand. Kazakh revolts which spread in the Russian rear among the nomads, like the Iset and Beket revolts of 1850–54 in the Middle Horde area, were suppressed without much difficulty.[2]

Thus, in the middle of the nineteenth century, the backward, medieval khanates of Khiva, Bukhara and Kokand, deprived of the protective buffer of the Kazakh Steppes, found themselves face to face with a great European power —Russia, ready and eager for an easy colonial acquisition.

The years 1854 and 1855 saw also the revival of the old Russian dream of invading India. Two highly ambitious projects were formulated in St. Petersburg concerning a possible expedition. These plans, however, were rendered impossible through the Russian defeat in the Crimean War in 1855.

The Conquest

The three khanates of Turkestan facing Russian colonial conquest had no well-defined borders. The Emir of Bukhara ruled a large territory between the Syr-Darya and Amu-Darya rivers, with the exception of a vast desert area south of the Aral Sea. The heart of his country was the rich valley of Zeravshan with the historic cities of Bukhara and Samarkand. The country had a population of about two and one-half million, half of them Uzbeks, one-third Tajiks and about one-tenth Turkmen.

The lands of the Khan of Khiva were located south of the Aral Sea, on both shores of the Amu-Darya, with the oasis of Khiva in the center. Its population was about three-quarters of a million and consisted of Kara-Kalpaks, Turkmen, Kazakhs and Uzbeks.

Kokand occupied vast territories between the Syr-Darya and the Chinese Sinkiang, with the center in the rich Fergana valley and in the Tashkent oasis. With a population of about three million, mostly Uzbeks, Kazakhs and Kirgizes, it included the largest city in Central Asia, Tashkent (one hundred thousand inhabitants).

Nomad Turkmen, between the Caspian Sea and the Amu-Darya river, and those Kazakhs in the northern steppes who were not yet under Russian protection recognized the authority of the khans only intermittently.

The political and social structure of the three khanates was medieval. The land, divided into three main categories—state (*amliak*), private (*miulk*), and clerical (*vakf*)—was most often cultivated by impoverished tenants who were allowed to retain only between one-half and one-fifth of the crop. Economic activity was mostly of a local character. Slavery existed throughout the territory. The military and the administrative organization of the khanates was backward, and only Khiva, because of its smaller territory, achieved a certain degree of centralization. The outlying provinces (*vilayets*) of Bukhara and Kokand were constantly challenging the central authority. Uzbek political supremacy in a multinational situation led to national conflicts. In addition, the three khans were usually quarreling with one another.

The Russians, avoiding direct hostile contact with Bukhara and Khiva (a mission was sent there in 1858), started a series of local operations at the Kokand borders. Moving south along the Syr-Darya river toward the Kirgiz mountains, they took Tokmak and Pishpek in 1860, Djulek and Yany-Kurgan in 1861, Turkestan City, Aulie-Ata and finally Chimkent in 1864. The local Russian field commander, General Chernyaev, established at Chimkent, tried to take Tashkent by surprise, but failed. The exasperated Kokand government was unwilling to relinquish its major centers, Tashkent and the Fergana valley, without a full-scale war. The Russians were ready. In 1865 they created a separate Turkestan province under the jurisdiction of the remote Orenburg governor-general. In June General Chernyaev, with 1,950 men and twelve cannons, marched on Tashkent and took the city by assault. The 30,000 Moslem defenders, with sixty-three cannons, were unable to inflict serious losses on the Russians. This victory had a demoralizing effect on the natives and enhanced Russian prestige. The Emir of Bukhara, frightened by Russian victories, finally decided to act. He asked the Russians to evacuate Tashkent and detained the Russian mission in Bukhara. At the same time the weak Khan of Kokand was replaced, with Bukhara's backing, by their choice, Khudoyar Khan. Armed Bukharan bands harassed Russian communications as far as Tashkent. In 1866 the Russians turned against Bukhara, beating Bukharan troops at Irdjar. They took Khodjent and Ura Tiube and defeated the Bukharans again at Yany-Kurgan. This was followed by a reorganization of the conquered territory. The Turkestan province was made into a separate governorship-general with the capital at Tashkent, and then divided into two provinces, Syr-Darya and Semirechye (1867). (In 1868 the Kazakh Steppes were also divided into Russian-style administrative units under military governors.) General Kaufman, the aggressive Russian army commander in the area, was made the first governor-general of Turkestan. In January, 1868, Kaufman concluded a peace treaty with Kokand, but pursued the fight against Bukhara. In May, with 3,500 men, he took the historic city of Samarkand almost without a fight and, following the course of the Zeravshan river, reached Katta-Kurgan. The Bukharan army, almost 50,000 strong, outflanked the Russians and attacked Samarkand, but failed to break the resistance of its 658-man garrison. In

June, Bukhara was forced to sign a peace treaty which made this khanate a vassal of Russia. Bukhara was also required to cede both Samarkand and Katta-Kurgan.

It was also at this time (1869) that Russian Caucasian troops crossed the Caspian Sea and established the fort and the harbor of Krasnovodsk. This served as the base for future advances across Turkmen desert. Only Khiva was left untouched; protected by arid deserts, she was still inaccessible.

In 1873, however, despite Russian peaceful declarations, General Kaufman moved against Khiva, entered the city and forced the Khan to accept a Russian protectorate (August, 1873). Included in the terms were the cession of the western part of his territory and the payment of a contribution. Simultaneously, acting from Krasnovodsk, Russian troops pacified the Caspian coast (1870–73).

Thus, eight years after the fall of Tashkent, all three khans of Turkestan had become vassals of Russia, and a large part of their territories had been made into a Russian province under the governorship of General Kaufman.

Widespread dissatisfaction with the new state of affairs led to a revolt against the unpopular Khudoyar Khan in Kokand. His son, Nasreddin, was proclaimed khan, and a holy war began against the Russians. Russian troops, under Colonel Skobelev, were quick to act. Skobelev defeated the natives at Makhram, entered the Fergana valley and took all the main cities of the valley one after another—Namangan, Andijan, Kokand, Margelan. In reprisal for the revolt, Russia incorporated the Khanate of Kokand into Russian Turkestan and exiled the unfortunate Khudoyar Khan (1876). In reward for his victories, Colonel Skobelev was promoted to general and made governor of the new Fergana province of Turkestan.

During the same year Russian troops pacified the Kirgiz tribes in the east and in 1877 took Kzyl-Arvat in

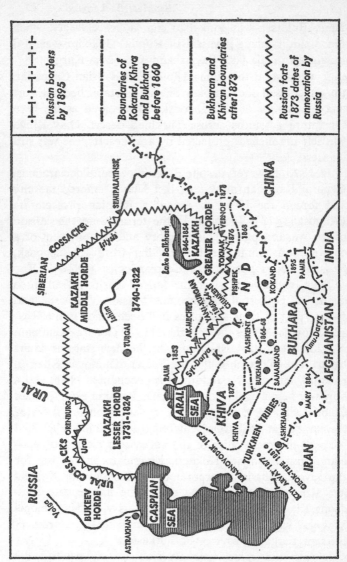

Russian Conquest of Central Asia

the Teke oasis of Turkmenia. Skobelev, proud of his success, submitted a plan of invasion of India to General Kaufman. However, having established herself in Central Asia, Russia was unwilling to risk a war with Britain by following Skobelev's aggressive plans. Britain acted swiftly: Queen Victoria was proclaimed "Empress of India" (1877) in a manifest indication of British intentions to stand firm in the area. This did not prevent the Russians from testing British patience at the Afghan borders. In 1878 General Stoletov of the Russian Transcaspian Force was sent with a diplomatic mission to Kabul. In 1879 Russian troops moved against the Teke Turkmen tribes, but then suffered a defeat at Geok-Tepe. Russian units were on the move in the entire area. Only the Congress of Berlin was able to call a halt to further Russian advance. However, the pacification of Turkmenia continued. In 1880 the Russians began to build a strategic railroad from the Caspian Sea to the hinterland, and a new expedition under General Skobelev was sent against the recalcitrant Teke Turkmen. Eleven thousand men attacked the fort of Geok-Tepe and, after a fierce battle, took it in January, 1881. This was the last large-scale battle of the campaign.

In 1881 the Russians created the Transcaspian province from the Turkmen territory and pushed the Transcaspian Railroad from the Caspian coast to Kzyl-Arvat.

General Kaufman died a year later, having witnessed the success of his policy. In 1884 the last strongholds of native resistance, the Turkmen oases of Mary and Tedjen, recognized Russian authority. A year later the Transcaspian Railroad had reached Mary. The conquest of Central Asia was achieved. Russia offered to trace a frontier with British-dominated Afghanistan. For that purpose a mixed English-Russian commission was set up. While the commission was still being formed, a clash occurred in March,

1855, at the Kushka river between Russians and Afghans led by British advisors. The conflict, however, was not allowed to get out of hand. In 1887 the border between Afghanistan and Russian Central Asia was finally determined.

By 1886 the Turkestan governorship-general was divided into three parts: the Syr-Darya province, the Fergana province and the Zeravshan district (since 1887, Samarkand province). The railroad reached Samarkand in 1888.[3] All of Central Asia was pacified, and the Moslem people of Central Asia were forced to accept the reality of Russian domination.

Tsarist Policy

Tsarist internal policy in Central Asia was calculated to ensure continued domination by keeping peace and order in the area and interfering as little as possible with the native customs and way of life. Soon, however, three problems emerged which were to dominate the development of the area. The first was the cotton boom in Turkestan. The needs of the Russian and Polish textile industry for cheap domestic cotton, the fertility of the rich soil of the Fergana valley and the successful introduction of American cotton (around 1884) in that area made cotton a key product. Second was the problem of so-called "surplus lands" in the Kazakh Steppe and in Kirgizia. There, the lands of the nomads, wherever suitable for agriculture, were bought, seized or expropriated by the Russians. The number of Russian settlers grew rapidly, while the natives, like the American Indians, were forced to move out into less desirable areas. The third problem was common to both Turkestan and the Steppe Region— the fact that Central Asia had become a choice market for Russian-manufactured goods. These three factors— cotton, surplus land and markets—were focal points for the years ahead. The total land under American cotton cultivation increased sixfold from 1886 to 1890. Imported cotton, free of duty until 1878, then taxed only 2.4 rubles per quintal, was hit with a 6-ruble import duty in 1887 and a 24-ruble levy in 1903. The Russian textile industry, which imported 96 per cent of all of Russia's cotton needs in 1886, was importing only 48.7 per cent by 1914. The rest was supplied by Central Asia, where the area under cotton cultivation grew from 13,200 hectares in 1886 to 597,200 hectares in 1914.[4]

The cotton boom had a decisive influence on other fields of activity. First, the increase of cotton production was combined with the growth of the grain deficit. Central Asia, previously self-supporting in grain, had to rely increasingly on grains imported from Russia. The industrial development was also centered around cotton. In fact, cotton mills employed two-thirds of all industrial workers and accounted for over three-fourths of the total industrial production of Central Asia in terms of value. While exporting cotton, Central Asia was increasing her import of Russian cotton textiles.

The cotton boom created a real basis for a money economy. Central Asian markets were opened to Russian industrial goods. Unable to compete with Western manufacturers on equal terms, Russian manufacturers were in need of a protected market with tariff barriers to check foreign competition. Central Asia was perfect in this respect. By 1907 she became an important buyer of grains, sugar, lumber, iron and steel products as well as of manufactured goods from metropolitan Russia.[5]

The problem of land surplus was the most complicated one. Prior to the 1861 abolition of serfdom in Russia, the only Russians settling in Kazakh territory were the free Cossacks, and they settled only along the lines of fortifications on the edge of the Kazakh Steppe. After the emancipation, peasants from Tomsk and Tobolsk provinces started to settle in Northern Kazakhstan. Peasants from the Samara, Saratov, Voronezh, Kursk, Kiev, Orel, Tambov, Chernigov and the Don provinces followed, especially after the 1891 famine. By 1893 the total number of newcomers reached 200,000.[6]

At this point, Russian authorities decided to give the colonization movement a more orderly character. A new ordinance in 1891 strengthened the Russian administrative hold in the steppe, and a special regulation was issued governing further colonization. The next Russian move was the sending of an expedition to the Kazakh steppe (1895) in order to establish a "land fund" for new settlers out of land "not needed" by the mostly nomad natives. This was the first organized step toward dispossessing the natives. The commission was not too careful in making distinctions between "needed" and "not needed" land. Pressure was applied to make the natives relinquish "superfluous" land. Russian immigration increased. Every spring, wagon loads of weary peasants crossed the Ural mountains and went down to the virgin lands of Kazakhstan in search of a new life.

In 1902 a new commission was sent to Turkestan. The commission found that large areas of land in the steppe of Semirechye were "not needed" by the natives and could qualify as surplus land. It was also understood that Russian farms needed much more land than native farms, because Russian peasants used extensive methods of agriculture and planted mainly grains.[7]

Until then, the number of Russian Cossacks and peasants in Semirechye was small (only 2,500 by 1883). There were also some workers who had remained in that area after the building of a canal, and refugees from the 1891–92 famine in Russia. The findings of the commission and the mass arrival of Russian peasants after the collapse of the 1905 Russian revolution led to an accelerated expropriation of native land. In 1908 a second commission was sent to the steppe, headed by Count K. K. Palen, which led to a new increase in Russian colonization. Thus, between 1903 and 1911, the Russian rural population of Semirechye increased from 95,000 to 175,000, and the number of Russian rural settlers in Syr-Darya region reached 45,000. The expropriation of Kazakh and Kirgiz lands was made easier by a legal device based on the highly questionable assumption that all the lands in the steppe formerly belonged to the khans and not to private owners, and therefore, after the Russian conquest the tsar became the rightful heir to all the legal titles to the land.[8]

The taking over of "surplus lands" was most often done under harsh administrative pressure, and resulted in forcing the natives out of their own land. Not only nomads, but even settled Kazakhs and Kirgizes were faced with these measures. The take-over of "surplus lands" was again accelerated after the visit to the area by Prime Minister P. A. Stolypin in 1910. It is estimated that between forty and forty-five million hectares of Kazakh land were taken over prior to the Revolution. The main areas of land seizures were western, northern and eastern Kazakhstan and, after 1905, Semirechye and Syr-Darya as well. The land expropriation resulted in yearly famines among the Moslems between 1910 and 1913.[9] The annual income of the average Russian farm was twice as large as that of an average Kazakh farm in that same area. The real difference was greater, however, since most of the Kazakh wealth was concentrated in the hands of tribal aristocracy, which accounted for less than 4 per cent of the total native population.

The expropriation of "surplus lands" continued after the beginning of World War I. In 1916 the tsarist government, in need of manpower, decided to draft Central

Asian Moslems, traditionally free from draft obligation, into labor units. This was the last straw. A revolt flared in Kazakhstan under the leadership of Amangeldy Imanov, Abdu Gafar Dzhambosyn and Kasym Ospan. The revolt spread to the Dzhizak district of Samarkand and to the Fergana valley. The total number of rebels may have reached 50,000 by October. In November they almost took the town of Turgai, but failed and returned to the steppes.[10]

Meanwhile a conference on the revolt was held by General Kuropatkin, governor-general of Turkestan. At this conference it was decided to expel from their land and into eastern Kirgizia all the natives who took part in the revolt. Their lands were to be opened to immediate Russian settlement. The resettlement decision was carried on while the revolt was still in progress. In fact, a few days before the February (1917) Revolution, Russian punitive troops were still pursuing the remnants of rebel units. A quarter of a million Kazakhs and Kirgizes fled to Chinese Turkestan or died of famine.[11] The termination of land expropriations and of Russian settlement of the area became the main aspiration of Kazakh and Kirgiz nationalists in the years to come.

Chapter 2

The Revolution

The Two Revolutions

"THE FEBRUARY REVOLUTION reached Turkestan by cable," states G. Safarov, the best authority for the revolutionary period.[1] General Kuropatkin, the tsarist governor-general of Turkestan, tried to cling to power, but was replaced by a committee of the provisional government composed of five Russians and four local Moslems. Almost simultaneously, a "Council (Soviet) of Workers and Soldiers" was set up in Tashkent similar in structure to the metropolitan Soviets. It comprised various left-wing elements, but mainly Mensheviks and Social Revolutionaries (SR's). Right-wing groupings countered this move by organizing "Committees of Public Safety" in several towns.

The Moslems had nothing to do with all this. Nationalist Moslems gathered around religious *Ulema* groups, the only ones expressing an open desire for independence. Liberal Moslem groups, unwilling to jeopardize the support of the new liberal Russian regime, avoided the issue. Extreme radicals among the Moslems were few, and these were represented by the small "Union of Toiling Moslems" in Samarkand and a similar minor group in Fergana.

Moslem congresses were called by Moslem nationalists in May and September. The May congress pronounced itself in favor of the creation of an autonomous federated republic of Turkestan (within the new Russia) based on national autonomy and *Shariat* (Moslem religious law). It was decided to stop the planting of American cotton, the growing of which was associated with colonialism.

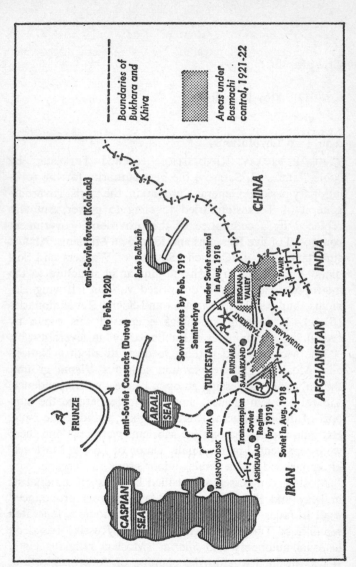

Civil War in Central Asia

The replacement of cotton by grains was equated with the liberation of Turkestan from economic dependence upon Russia.[2] The congress elected a Central Moslem Council with Mustafa Chokay as chairman. Chokay immediately began forwarding a series of demands to Tashkent. Included were the transfer of judiciary authority into Moslem hands and the abolition of separate European courts, electoral equality for Moslems and Russians, removal of Russian troops and establishment of an independent legislative assembly in Turkestan.

The Tashkent Committee of the provisional government, upon which these demands were made, was already on its way out. During September the soldiers of the two Siberian regiments stationed in Tashkent, with the leftist workers of the Tashkent Railroad Repair Shops, held a meeting. They demanded that essential goods be requisitioned from local capitalists, that workers be in control in factories, that banks be nationalized, and that power be transferred into the hands of the Tashkent Soviet.

The provisional government decided to react. General Korovnichenko, the commander of the Turkestan military district, was ordered to move his troops on Tashkent. Under his command armored trains and Cossack cavalry entered the city. An uneasy truce was established between Korovnichenko on one side and the Soviet, shielded by the two regiments of Siberian infantry, on the other. Korovnichenko was slowly gaining control when the Bolsheviks took power in Petrograd. This prompted Korovnichenko to force the issue. Two days later he had the Tashkent Soviet arrested and ordered the disarming of the pro-Soviet Siberian infantry. The first regiment, taken by surprise, was disarmed successfully, but the second, reinforced by railroad workers, met force with force. In the resulting fierce battle the Siberian units gained the upper hand, thereby restoring the Soviet to power.

The Menshevik-SR Soviet, once again in command, refused to recognize the new Bolshevik regime in Petrograd. To strengthen its prestige among the Moslems, the Soviet established two organizations with resounding names and a minimum of authority: the Executive Committee and the Krai-Soviet (territorial council), in both of which the nationalist *Ulema* Moslems were given half the seats.

Within the Soviet, Bolsheviks, Mensheviks and SR's (Social Revolutionaries) were quarreling. The Bolsheviks wanted to set up a purely proletarian regime as in metropolitan Russia. In an area where the only organized proletariat was Russian and where the mass of local population consisted of small proprietors—peasants, artisans, and small merchants—such a dogma had a strong flavor of colonialism.[3] The moderately socialist Mensheviks advocated local autonomy based on a large degree of self-government for local authorities and on universal suffrage. The left-wing SR's were interested in a peasant government which, under local conditions, would have amounted to government by the rural Russian settlers of Semirechye. The settlers of Semirechye, in turn, wanted either autonomy or union with Siberian anti-Communists. The Bolshevik minority in the Soviet was unwilling to accept the policies of the Menshevik-SR majority or to tolerate the sharing of power with the Moslem nationalists, even on paper. On November 19, 1917, the Bolsheviks created their own government and a rival of the Tashkent Soviet, the Council of People's Commissars, composed of seven Bolsheviks and one left-wing SR. All were Russians.

Moslem nationalists were quick to follow. Their Fourth All-Moslem Congress met in Kokand on November 26 and 27 and created the Moslem Provisional Government of Autonomous Turkestan with Tamyshbaev as premier and Chokaev as minister of foreign affairs. The Kokand cabinet included one non-Moslem, the finance minister

Herzfeld. However, the new Moslem government, the third contender for power in Turkestan, lacked both troops and money and consequently was unable to back its bid for power with necessary force.

The course of events in the Kazakh Steppe did not favor the Moslems either. The February Revolution found them divided between the liberal-nationalist Alash-Orda party (Mirzhakup Dulatov, Alikhan Bukheikhanov and Baitursunov), which received the support of the provisional government, and the radical elements who had survived the Russian suppression of the 1916 revolt (Amangeldy Imanov and others). The few local leftists, such as Dzhangeldyn, joined the radicals.

A number of Kazakhs and Kirgizes, who fled the country after the 1916 revolt, started to return to their former homes. Their former properties were, however, already occupied by Russian settlers. Serious strife developed between the returning natives and the new settlers, who preferred the use of force to the surrendering of their recently acquired property. Local Russian garrisons, poorly disciplined, ineffectually tried to keep some semblance of peace.

During this period two Kazakh congresses had been held in Orenburg. Through this medium the Kazakh nationalist party, Alash-Orda, formulated new demands: expulsion of Russian settlers, termination of draft and return to native administration of education. The emerging idea of national autonomy had little time to develop. The success of the October Revolution threw the whole area into a new turmoil.

The Struggle for Survival

The young Soviet regime in Turkestan was almost immediately cut off from Soviet Russia by the anti-Communist Cossack troops of Ataman Dutov, and remained so, with a few short interruptions, until the fall of 1919. The only solid support for the new regime came from the Russian workers of the Tashkent Railroad Repair Shops and the troops of the local garrison.

On December 13, Mohammed's birthday, the Moslem nationalists organized a demonstration in Tashkent in which some Russian anti-Communists participated also. The soldiers dispersed the demonstrators, killing eighteen people in the process, but renewed recognition had been won, as the Tashkent Council of People's Commissars decided to appease the Moslems by offering to call a Turkestan constituent assembly.

Meantime, the Kokand Moslem government, plagued by the lack of military force and in need of military alliances, decided to join the "Southeastern Union of Cossacks, Mountain Caucasians and Peoples of the Steppe." This organization had been created on paper by the anti-Communist General Kaledin. As the latter, busy with his own problems, supplied no troops, the Kokand government made an "opening to the left" by giving one-third of the seats in its Moslem Congress to the freshly organized Kokand Moslem Soviet, a left-wing organization modeled on the Russian Soviets of Workers' and Soldiers' Deputies.

While the Kokand government was maneuvering for support, anti-Communist Cossack troops finally began moving eastward from the Caspian Sea toward Tashkent. The Tashkent Soviet threw its military forces against the Cossacks and routed them near Samarkand. Freed from that menace, the Tashkent Soviet finally decided to liquidate its embarrassing Moslem competitor. Soviet troops returning from Samarkand were ordered to Kokand. The Kokand government reacted by attacking the small Russian garrison within the city in the hope of destroying it before the arrival of the main Soviet force. This action was unsuccessful, and, in the meantime, the Soviet troops under Commissar Perfilev—consisting mostly of shabby units fresh from their Samarkand victory—reached the city. The hastily assembled defenders were made up of local Uzbek inhabitants, as well as some Teke-Turkmen, Caucasian Lezgin mountaineers and a few Persians, reinforced by local Moslem guerrillas under Irgash-bey. To further confuse the whole affair, the weak Kokand Moslem Soviet made an eleventh-hour attempt to take power in Kokand, hoping thereby to deprive the Russian troops of their reason for attack. The attempt failed and the Soviet troops assaulted the city on February 5 supported by a local Russian and Armenian mob. The Moslem defenders were routed. A real "pogrom" ensued, accompanied by looting and rape. The local Moslem population became deeply alienated from the Soviets.

The Tashkent Soviet made no attempt to win back the Moslems. During the winter famine of 1917–18 no effort was made to relieve the urban Moslem population with the requisite foodstuffs. In the villages Russian troops requisitioned food in what was, at that time, the accepted "war Communism" pattern. All cotton was surrendered under penalty of death. Moslem peasants suspected of sympathy with the nationalist guerrillas were shot. The Russian revolutionary slogan *svoboda* (freedom) became known among the Moslems as *svobodka* (little freedom) and given the meaning of lawlessness and looting.[4] The result was pitiful: all the countryside, cities and railroads were soon in Irgash-bey's hands.[5] The basis for the future nationalist Basmachi revolt was laid.

The next step of the Tashkent Soviet was an attempt to penetrate Bukhara, where the Emir maintained his authority undisturbed by the two revolutions in Russia. On February 28, 1918, the chairman of the Turkestan Council of People's Commissars, Kolesov, arrived in Bukhara from Tashkent to visit the Emir. As he expected, his demands for cooperation were rejected by the Emir. However, Kolesov had carefully stationed his troops in advance, should military action against Bukhara be necessary. His attack on March 2 routed the Bukharan defenders, and the Soviet troops penetrated the city. Again, as they had in Kokand, the troops looted the city. At this point the outraged population decided to back up the otherwise unpopular Emir, and the invaders were, in their turn, routed. Several hundred innocent Russian inhabitants of Bukhara were then slaughtered by the Moslem mob before the Emir's troops could intervene and stop the massacre.

The Soviet setback was followed by the signing of an agreement between the Emir of Bukhara and the Soviet regime of Tashkent for the recognition of Bukharan independence by the latter. In return, the Emir agreed to turn over anti-Communist Russian agents to the Soviets and to exchange prisoners without compensation. The truce was clearly a temporary solution, as the Emir continued to help the nationalist bands operating in Russian Turkestan and the Tashkent Soviet continued to plot the Emir's overthrow with the Bukharan radical groups.[6]

During that period the old Russian puppet, Khan Isfendiar, was deposed in Khiva by a very energetic opponent, Djunaid-Khan (January, 1918). Djunaid put his own man on the Khivan throne and established contact with both the Emir in Bukhara and the Basmachis in Russian Turkestan. In May he executed several left-wing Young Khivan leaders who were plotting against his regime.[7]

To a large extent these setbacks were due to the internal difficulties of the Tashkent Soviet government. Not only was the entire area in a state of economic collapse—a condition not helped by wholesale nationalization—but the popularity of the Tashkent Soviet authority among the

Moslems and among many Russian settlers was at a very low ebb.

To remedy the situation, Moscow sent an "extraordinary commissar" to Turkestan, a Russian Communist, P. A. Kobozev, to look into the situation. Under his guidance the Fifth Congress of Soviets in Tashkent proclaimed Turkestan part of the Russian Republic and elected a new government, containing eighteen Bolsheviks and eighteen left-wing SR's, with Kobozev himself as chairman.

In May events were more favorable for the Soviets. The Russian settlers of Semirechye finally decided to move against the anti-Communist Cossacks and create a Soviet regime in that area. This strengthened the position of the Tashkent Soviet, but the new Soviet regime of Semirechye proved to be a rather embarrassing ally, as Semirechye authorities were ridden with anti-Moslem and anti-Semitic prejudices, issued their own currency guaranteed by stocks of opium and favored the distilling of bootlegged vodka.

In Tashkent, Russian and Armenian nationalists, regardless of political allegiance, began to gather around the local Soviet regime as the only remaining "European" force in a sea of discontented natives. The struggle in Turkestan was followed along ever increasing nationalist lines with the Moslems pitted against the Russians. Concepts such as revolution and Communism were no longer of prime importance.

The number of Communists in Tashkent was nominal; the First Party Conference, which took place in June, 1918, counted only 250 party members in the entire city. This conference made a few empty gestures toward the Moslem masses. It "recognized" the Uzbek language as equal to Russian and expressed "confidence" in the Uzbek proletariat.[8]

The same month an anti-Soviet revolt started in the main city of Turkmenia, Ashkhabad. Tashkent sent an extraordinary commissar, Frolov, who succeeded only in making the situation worse. Local Turkmen tribesmen and anti-Communist Russian officers took over. The Transcaspian Soviet government was arrested and shot. Supported by British funds, an anti-Bolshevik Transcaspian government was set up to include anti-Communist Russians, Armenians and Turkmen. Soviet troops were soon ejected from the Mary oasis.

Soviet Turkestan was in a difficult position, caught between the Russian anti-Communist forces in Orenburg and those in the Turkmen steppes, the Cossacks pressing on Semirechye and the Moslem nationalist Basmachi revolt brewing in the valley of Fergana. In addition, the Soviet regime was affected by constant internal struggle. First, the left-wing SR's split with the Bolsheviks at the Sixth Congress of Soviets (Tashkent, October, 1918); then old and young Communists divided at the Second Party Congress (December, 1918). In December the Basmachi showed a considerable growth in strength. Then an anti-Communist revolt by Russian settlers had to be quelled in the Belovodsk district of Semirechye. On the night of January 18, 1919, events turned again for the worst, as the military commissar of the Tashkent Soviet government, Osipov, attempted to take over the city. Even though the revolt failed and the defeated Osipov fled to Bukhara, morale fell very low, especially since the workers of the Tashkent Railroad Repair Shops had taken part in the attempted coup.

In February, Moscow appointed a special temporary commission for Turkestan affairs. In addition to P. A. Kobozev, who was already heading the Tashkent Soviet government, two more Communist officials were sent from Moscow, S. Z. Eliava and A. S. Kiselev. Meanwhile, the situation in Khiva was getting tense. Since the middle of 1919 the Young Khivan and other anti-Djunaid elements were allowed to gather on the Soviet side of the border. Tashkent, nevertheless, aware of its own weakness, felt it necessary at this time to sign a treaty with Djunaid-Khan recognizing Khivan independence (April 9, 1919). The Soviet delegation sent to Khiva was officially headed by a former Turkish officer, Mohammed Kazembek. The real head of the Soviet delegation was, however, a Russian Communist, Khristoforov, who divided his attention between his official work in the delegation and behind-the-scene propaganda activities against Djunaid-Khan.[9] He remained in Khiva as Tashkent's envoy, but persisted in his intrigues and finally perished at the hands of Djunaid-Khan's men.

In the meantime a struggle between the pro-Moslem and colonialist factions was brewing in Tashkent. During the Seventh Congress of Soviets, after the left-wing SR's united with the Communists, a national section was created within the Party where Moslem Communists were at last given a chance to express their views. However, natives pursuing the goal of self-determination, such as the Kirgiz, T. Ryskulov, and the Uzbek, Tursun Khodzhaev, were not always sure enough of their safety to attend Party meetings without safe-conduct passes, which were necessary in order to avoid arbitrary arrests by Russian chauvinists active within the Tashkent Soviet regime.

A fight between the pro-Moslems and the colonialists finally took place at the Third Congress of the Communist Party of Turkestan. While Moscow's Commissar Kobozev sided with the pro-Moslems, Kazakov, the new head of the Tashkent government, sided with the colonialists. One of the leaders of the colonialists was Uspensky, a former member of the Black Hundreds (a violently reactionary organization), turned Communist. The Tashkent Soviet also took the side of the colonialists. In order to overcome their opposition, Kobozev had a new Turkestan

Party Committee elected which included seven Russians and three Moslems. The new Party Committee immediately clashed with the Tashkent government, while local Soviet authorities as well as the security forces continued to display their usual anti-Moslem bias. On July 12, 1919, Moscow cabled Tashkent demanding that Moslems be admitted into government bodies. On receiving the cable, Kazakov called a joint meeting of the heads of all the leading Soviet, Party and governmental institutions in Tashkent. The result of the meeting was a victory for the colonialists. A reply was sent to Moscow stating that owing to local conditions the admission of Moslems into local government bodies was impossible. It was also decided not to publish the contents of the Moscow cable.[10]

In September, 1919, two congresses met in Tashkent: the Eighth Congress of Soviets and the Fourth Congress of the Communist Party of Turkestan. From these congresses came the organization of the *Kombedy* (committees of poor peasants) in the usual Communist manner and the introduction of a state grain monopoly. Once again the new developments became a tool in the hands of Russian settlers and an excuse to confiscate food from the Moslem peasants. The Congress of Soviets was finally induced, however, to give the natives a majority in the Tashkent government.

In contrast with the political and economic dilemmas, the military situation had improved considerably. The Russian anti-Communist forces had been thrown out of Turkmenia (July, 1919). Admiral Kolchak was finally defeated in Siberia, and Turkestan was no longer isolated from the rest of the country.

The Revolution Expanded

The arrival of Soviet troops from the north, which followed the re-establishment of communications between

Turkestan and Russia proper, shifted the center of political power in Tashkent from the local authorities into the hands of Moscow's delegates and the military command of the freshly arrived Fourth Red Army. The Fourth Army Party Conference decided to overrule previous decisions of Tashkent authorities concerning the non-participation of Moslems in local Soviet organizations. In October, 1919, a commission for Turkestan affairs was established by a Moscow decree signed by Lenin. No Moslems were included. S. Z. Eliava, a Georgian, was named chairman and in charge of external relations. V. V. Kuybyshev and M. V. Frunze were concerned with military matters, Y. E. Rudzutak with economic problems, and F. I. Goloshchekin with party affairs. Also included was G. I. Bokii. They began to arrive in Tashkent in November, 1919. The Army Special (police) Section took over the local *Cheka* (political police). The ministry of foreign affairs of Turkestan, a symbol of far-reaching regional autonomy, was abolished and its functions transferred to the department of external relations within the commission itself. All supplies were channeled through the supply commission of the army, cutting the ground from under the feet of the Tashkent authorities.

In an attempt to stop the growth of Moscow's control in local Turkestan affairs, Russian settlers in and around Tashkent, including Communists, began to advocate local autonomy and to court the favor of local Moslems. The situation had improved, however. The Fifth Turkestan Party Conference elected Tursun Khodzhaev, a native Moslem, as first secretary. The Fourth Army headquarters, the Tashkent government and the Commission for Turkestan were now courting the favor of the Moslem majority. The commission sent a project to Moscow harshly criticizing the previous activities of the Soviet regime in Turkestan. The latter was said to have been infected with "colonialist psychology," and the local Moslem population was said to condemn their policies as "a continuation of the actions of the agents of the old tsarist regime."[11]

Following the commission's recommendations, Moscow pressed for action on two main goals: elimination of colonialist attitudes among Russian settlers and of "feudal-patriarchal attitudes" among the Moslems. Land taken from the Kirgizes after the suppression of the 1916 revolt was to be given back. Landless peasants, regardless of nationality, were to be given land. To implement this policy, Russian settlers were to be disarmed. Speculators, former bourgeois, former tsarist policemen and those among the old tsarist bureaucrats "who did not fit in the new Turkestan" were to be expelled and sent to concentration camps in Russia. Local Russian Communists with "colonialist mentality" were to be transferred to Russia and replaced by Communists from metropolitan Russia. Russians and Moslems were to be treated equally in the distribution of supplies by the state. This fresh approach was easy to proclaim, but difficult, if not impossible, to implement.

The Commission for Turkestan Affairs, which had been so critical of colonialists and their methods, soon reverted to the very position it had previously condemned. A conflict developed between the commission and the Moslem Communists of the Ryskulov group. The latter were this time backed by both the Party and the governmental authorities in Tashkent, where Moslems were now in the majority. Ryskulov, a friend of the Tatar nationalist-Communist foe of Stalin, Mir Sajit Sultan Galiev,[12] wanted it clearly understood that the arrival of the Fourth Red Army was not to be interpreted as a conquest of the area by Russian troops from metropolitan Russia. Ryskulov was opposed also to the idea of carrying the class struggle into the native community, especially during the period of decolonization. Unable to reach a working agreement with the commission, Ryskulov's groups resigned from the government. A new Tashkent government was organized with the more docile Rakhimbabaev as chairman. He and a score of cooperative native Communists were elected to the new Temporary Central Party Committee of Turkestan.

Moscow, aware of the difficulties in Tashkent, decided to send a new commission which again contained no Moslems and consisted of Sokolnikov, Safarov, Kaganovich and Peters. Under their auspices the Fifth Congress of the Communist Party of Turkestan and the Ninth Congress of Soviets (September, 1920) reaffirmed the principle of class struggle within the native Moslem masses, thus rejecting Ryskulov's contention of community of interest between the bourgeoisie and the proletariat of a colonized nation. Shortly thereafter Ryskulov, at the First Congress of the Peoples of the East in Baku, continued to advocate his and Sultan Galiev's ideas of the necessity of a bourgeois nationalist revolution in the colonial East, by arguing that the native proletariat in colonial areas was still much too weak to become a leading revolutionary force.[13]

As has since been demonstrated, both Sultan Galiev and Ryskulov were about thirty-five years in advance of their time and geographically misplaced. Only after Stalin's death, and then only in regard to Western colonial and underdeveloped areas, did Moscow accept their proposals as exemplifying the correct approach for the decolonization stage.

During 1920 things in Central Asia went quite differently. Even Safarov, the most pro-Moslem member of the new commission and an opponent of Ryskulov, soon found himself in conflict with his Russian colleagues. Letters were exchanged with Moscow leaders, involving Lenin, who grew suspicious of the Russian chauvinistic tendencies displayed by Russian officials in Tashkent, including the new chairman of the commission, M. P. Tomsky, and a member of that same group, the Latvian Communist, Peters.[14]

In the meantime, with the civil war ending, the Soviets decided to reorganize Khiva along more convenient lines. Even before the arrival of the Fourth Red Army, local Soviet authorities had reached a behind-the-scene agreement with Djunaid-Khan's feudal rivals. In November, 1919, a revolt began against Djunaid, led by another Turkmen chieftain, Gochmamed-Khan, which continued until the middle of December. By that time, the Soviets realized the inability of the rebels to win without direct Russian support, so on December 25, Soviet troops crossed the Khivan borders. Three days later Gochmamed-Khan became their official ally. After a month of resistance, Djunaid-Khan, with four hundred men, fled to the Kara-Kum desert. The legal ruler of Khiva, Djunaid's puppet Seid-Adulla, acquiesced to the new state of affairs. Despite his submission, he was deposed on February 2, 1920, and replaced by a pro-Soviet revolutionary committee. Djunaid-Khan made a comeback trying to take Khiva, but was repulsed.

On April 4, Khiva, already under Soviet control, was transformed into the People's Republic of Khorezm. In May this first Soviet satellite received its first Soviet envoy, Josif Moiseevich Byk.[15] Byk arrived to find that the newly created Khorezm government consisted not of genuine Communists, but of patriotic Young Khivan radicals. Two Young Khivans, Palvanniaz Yusupov and Sultanmuradov, had become respectively head of the government and head of the revolutionary committee. The only reliable man in the Khivan (Khorezm) government was old Djunaid's rival, Gochmamed-Khan, who became the deputy chairman of the revolutionary committee. The People's Republic of Khorezm duly signed a treaty of alliance with Soviet Russia (September, 1920). Nevertheless, a serious conflict was developing between the nationalist-minded Young Khivans and their Russian "protectors."[16]

Having established a People's Republic in Khiva, the Soviet government decided to follow a similar approach to Bukhara. On March 14, 1920, M. V. Frunze, the commander of the Turkestan Red Army, visited the Emir, repeating the 1918 attempt by Kolesov to persuade him to "cooperate" with the Soviets.[17] This démarche, made only five weeks after the Soviets' take-over of Khiva, was bound to fail and brought no positive results whatsoever. On the contrary, the Emir sent an emissary to London in an attempt to obtain British support. He also contacted anti-Soviet Moslem guerrilla leaders from neighboring Soviet areas.

Having failed to achieve his objectives by negotiation, Frunze decided to act. Russian workers staged a revolt in a Bukharan town on the Turkestan-Bukharan border. Simultaneously the small revolutionary Young Bukharan group started a revolt in Bukhara itself, and, as in 1918, Russian troops were ready in advance. But this time they were not poorly disciplined Red Guards from Tashkent, but regular units of Commander Frunze's army. They crossed the Bukharan border on the same day and after a four-day battle took Bukhara (September, 1920). The Emir fled south to the Tajik mountains and the People's Republic of Bukhara was established. Frunze, his task accomplished, was transferred to the Ukraine to command Soviet operations against the anti-Communist forces in the Crimea.

Ten days later V. Kuibyshev arrived in Bukhara as the first official envoy of Moscow. The assignment of such a prominent Soviet leader to this position speaks for itself. Kuibyshev was not sent to Bukhara merely to be an envoy —he intended to rule.

On November 3, 1920, a treaty of military, political and economic cooperation was signed between Moscow and the newly established Bukharan government, and in December Soviet troops started to move toward eastern Bukhara to throw out the Emir.[18] Emir Said Alim Khan, who fled to Diushambe (today Tajik's capital) was unable to resist. On the tenth of March he crossed the border to Afghanistan.[19]

Soviet domination over the area seemed to be secure at this point, but new obstacles—national Communism in both Khiva and Bukhara, and the Moslem nationalist revolt all over the area—were already looming in the path of the Soviet regime.

Chapter 3

The Basmachi Revolt

THE WORD *basmach,* which originally meant "bandit," was not new in Central Asia. Bandits had always roamed the countryside, attacking and plundering caravans, and had been especially brazen during troubled times. The Moslem nationalist Kokand government, before collapsing, had received the support of the local Basmachi leader, Irgash-bey. Later, some members of the Kokand government fled to the Basmachi, giving an ideological and patriotic coloring to its activity. Organized around local leaders, the growth of the Basmachi movement was similar to that in Algeria of the 1950's, where the term *fellagha* (peasant) originally used by the French to describe Algerian bandits, changed into that of a nationalist patriot waging a war of liberation against colonial oppression. The impetus for the growth of the Basmachi movement was twofold: a struggle for national independence resulting from the destruction by the Soviets of the Kokand Moslem government and subsequent colonial-like outrages, and the economic crisis stemming from the ruin of cotton crops in the Fergana valley,[1] with its attendant famine.

The initial phase of the Basmachi revolt took place from February, 1918, when the Moslem Kokand government was overthrown, to September, 1920, when Soviet troops seized Bukhara. The Basmachi were active mostly in the Fergana valley during this period. The blunders made by the Tashkent Soviet government tended to work for the Basmachi. Requisitions for bread and cotton, the shooting of Moslem peasants suspected of being sympathetic to the Basmachi and the looting by poorly disciplined Red troops played in favor of the Basmachi. Such slogans as "Turkestan for the Turks" and "Turkestan without violence" were popular among the native Moslem population. Many native Soviet officials defected. One of them, Madamin-bek, the head of the Soviet militia in the Fergana valley town of Margelan, became a prominent Basmachi leader and a rival to Irgash-bey. In November, 1918, he and an allied Basmachi group of Khal-Hodja's attacked the villages of Russian settlers in the valley. Local Russian settlers, in an attempt to fend off further raids, created an army of their own, and this army received official recognition and support from the Fergana Red Army headquarters. However, under the impact of the unpopular Soviet decree establishing the state grain monopoly, the Fergana peasant army began to grow restless. The Soviets, aware of this, tried to disarm them in June, 1919, but failed. This in turn alienated the settlers.

In August the settlers' army demanded civil rights and the abolition of state grain monopolies and revolutionary tribunals. The Basmachi chieftain, Madamin-bek, supported these demands and joined his seven-thousand-man force to the peasant army. Their combined forces took the town of Osh in September. A temporary government for Fergana was created with Madamin-bek as chairman and military commander, and, as deputy chairman, Konstantin Monstrov, a former Soviet staff officer and the commander of the settlers' army. A joint Moslem and Russian anti-Communist force seemed to be in the making in Fergana.

Soon, however, the entire military picture changed. Soviet metropolitan troops, led by Army Commander Michael Frunze, arrived in Turkestan. The Soviet regime in Tashkent was no longer isolated from the rest of Soviet Russia. Fresh Soviet troops were sent to Fergana valley, and by the end of September they had retaken the few towns which had previously fallen into rebel hands. During this time, the relations between the Russian settlers and the Basmachi had been deteriorating. In January, Monstrov and his men surrendered to the Red Army. In a brilliant political move the Moslem Volga Tatar Red brigade was sent to subdue the Basmachi. The latter began to surrender in large numbers: twenty-six hundred in January, three thousand in February. Those remaining were crushed on February 4. By the middle of March, 1920, Madamin himself was forced to surrender. Only one important Basmachi chieftain, Kur-Shirmat, remained in the field. The revolt in Fergana valley appeared to be at an end. Former Basmachi units were transformed into "Soviet Basmachi" units of the First Uzbek Cavalry brigade.[2]

The second period of the Basmachi revolt started with the Soviet military actions against Khiva and Bukhara. In April, 1920, the People's Republic of Khorezm (Khiva) was proclaimed. In September the Emir of Bukhara fled to Diushambe and, in turn, the People's Republic of Bukhara was established. Although the Emir was unable to remain in Diushambe and was forced to take refuge in Afghanistan (March, 1921), his departure only increased nationalist resistance. Mullah Abdul-Kahar was appointed by the Emir to head the resistance in Bukhara. Soviet attempts to induce, by negotiation, the remnants of Basmachi forces in the Fergana valley to surrender also failed.

The Soviet take-over in Bukhara irritated the natives all over Central Asia. The action of Russian food-requisition squads and the untimely mobilization (summer, 1920) of Moslem conscripts into the Soviet army resulted in mass desertion of Moslems over to the Basmachi. Basmachi forces began to grow from day to day. Moslem Red Army units were increasingly unreliable. An order was given to disarm the First Uzbek Cavalry brigade. The result was grave. The brigade (with few exceptions) joined the Basmachi. Under the leadership of a local chieftain, Kur-Shirmat, Basmachi strength increased. They were a force of six thousand who knew the area, had an effective intelligence service, and, what is most important, had the support of the local population. In the event of defeat they could disappear in the villages. As a result, all Fergana valley was under their control. The Soviets dominated only the main cities and railroads.[3]

On February 22, 1921, G. V. Zinoviev, head of the anti-Basmachi operations in Fergana, met with the Basmachi representatives in the Fergana valley, but failed to obtain their surrender.[4] In April, the Soviet situation temporarily improved. A Basmachi chieftain, Dzhany-bek, went over to their side. From his followers and from the remnants of the First Uzbek Cavalry brigade a native regiment was formed. The winter of 1920–21 was severe. People became weary. In August and September, peace parleys were held between the Soviets and the Basmachi, and the prospects for peace appeared encouraging.[5] Meanwhile, hungry Russian refugees poured into the area.[6] Elsewhere in Central Asia the situation was also very difficult. In Kazakhstan, despite aid from the American Relief Administration and the relaxation of economic pressures due to the introduction of the New Economic Policy (NEP), both the famine and the Basmachi were spreading.[7]

In Khiva, the local Communist Party was becoming more and more nationalistic. Gochmamed-Khan, the leading local Soviet supporter, was shot. As a result, serious difficulties developed between his Turkmen followers and the Uzbek nationalist-Communists, who were in power. Khivan authorities gave refuge to the Bashkir Moslem nationalist, Zeki Validov (November, 1920), who had fled there after the liquidation by the Russians of the Volga Bashkir autonomy.

The Commission for Turkestan Affairs in Tashkent and Kuibyshev in Bukhara could no longer tolerate this state of affairs. In January a large group of Party men, headed by a Russian Communist, Safonov, arrived in Khiva on Kuibyshev's orders. Khivan Communists tried to discredit Safonov in Moscow by alleging that he used violence in dealing with Moslem Communists, but their efforts failed and the integration of Khiva proceeded as planned by Tashkent. The political department of the Soviet Khivan Red Army assumed responsibility for the Party work in Khiva supplanting the nationalist Central Committee. Finally, on the night of March 14, 1921, the Young Khivan government was deposed. Its members fled into the desert and joined their former enemy, Djunaid-Khan. The Soviets set up a new, more obedient, Khivan government. A Party purge followed. Of two thousand Party members, only sixty were judged reliable enough to retain their Party cards. The Republic's name was transformed from People's Republic to Soviet Republic, an important step forward on the road to complete integration.[8]

The result of the Khivan putsch intensified Moslem nationalist resistance to the Soviets in Bukhara. The Lokai valley of Gissar became a hotbed of new Basmachi revolt. Ibragim-bek, a member of a local Uzbek tribe, organized the main Basmachi forces. New Basmachi chieftains arose both in the Tapik mountains and in the Fergana valley (Kur-Shirmat, Rakhman-Datkho, Khal-Hodja, Nurmat-Ali and others). The flag of the Moslem nationalist revolt was hoisted over Central Asia.

The Soviets took drastic steps to stop the spreading of the rebellion. S. S. Kamenev, the commander-in-chief of the Red Army, arrived in Central Asia to set up campaign plans against the Basmachi. In January, 1922, an extraordinary dictatorial commission for East-Bukharan affairs, with full powers in that area, was established by the "People's Government" of Bukhara[9] and it remained in force until May 28, 1924. At the same time, the Central Committee of the Communist Party in Moscow organized a special commission, consisting of I. V. Stalin (then People's Commissar for Nationalities), G. V. Chicherin (People's Commissar for Foreign Affairs) and V. V. Kuibyshev (who arrived from Central Asia), to study the materials presented by the Commission for Turkestan Affairs concerning the situation in Bukhara. The Commission acted rapidly.

In February the Bukharan Communist Party was brought under the control of the Russian Communist Party. All the anti-Basmachi operations in Bukhara, Fergana and elsewhere in Turkestan were unified. Validov, already expelled from Khiva, and other Bashkir and Tatar Moslem nationalists were expelled from Bukhara.[10]

National Communism was, however, as strong among Young Bukharans as it had been among the Young Khivans. The newly organized satellite government of the People's Republic of Bukhara was torn between satisfaction at having eliminated the feudal regime of the Emir and the nationalist aspirations for more independence from the Russians. At the same time, on Moscow's instigation, Enver Pasha, one of the leaders of the defunct Young Turkish Government of Turkey, was sent to Bukhara. Son-in-law of the last sultan, army general, revolutionary and adventurer, he arrived on November 8, 1921, looked into the local situation and soon decided to change sides. Enver, having left his former Soviet friends, reached the Emir and was appointed commander-in-chief of his (or rather, Basmachi) forces in the field. The latter were, at that time, accumulating successes. In February a former Young Bukharan, Usman Hodja, head of the government of the Bukharan People's Republic, arrived in Diushambe with six hundred men. Dissatisfied with the Soviet policy, he reached an agreement with the Basmachi and took over the town, overwhelming the malaria-ridden Soviet garrison. The Bukharan People's Commissars of War and of the Interior also went to the Basmachi side. The Basmachi force, already twenty thousand men strong in December, 1921, was growing, and the local population was giving its support to them.[11] Moslem nationalist agitation was spreading even in Tashkent. In December the Soviets arrested the illegal Moslem Committee of National Union, operating since February in Tashkent and headed by the Tashkent Mufti.[12]

The struggle between the Basmachi and the Soviet Russian troops was not between Communists and anti-Communists, as in Russia, but between Russians and Moslems. The Basmachi, despite some initial short-term opportunistic alliances with anti-Communist Russian groups, was a native Moslem Turkestani movement. The Soviet troops fighting the Basmachi were, on the contrary, metropolitan troops of Russian nationality (with some Ukrainians and Tatars added). Native Turkestani soldiers were very few, their proportion less than that of Moslems in the French troops in Algeria. Uzbeks accounted for less than 5 per cent in 1927, while Kirgizes, Turkmen and other natives numbered altogether even less than that.[13] Even this small percentage was reached only after a big effort was made, in 1926, to create some native Turkestani Soviet units. From 1920 to 1926, during the crucial years of the revolt, the percentage of native soldiers in the Red Army in Turkestan was even less significant.

During the spring of 1922 the revolt was approaching a climax. The government of the People's Republic of Bukhara, after the defection of Usman Hodja, was headed by Faizulla Khodzhaev, a former member of the 1918 Kolesov expedition against Bukhara, and by Arifov, a nationalist Communist who was not too willing to pursue the fight against the Basmachi with the requisite determination. The situation was getting dangerous for the Soviets, as they were faced with growing Basmachi strength and with nationalistic tendencies among the Moslem Communists. The satellite government of Bukhara was forced to call for immediate Russian military assistance.[14]

In February a strong Basmachi force, under Mullah Abdul-Kahar, started a revolt near Bukhara, endangering the security of the city.[15] Faced with an increasingly dangerous situation, the Soviets decided to take drastic steps. In March their war effort was subjected to a complete reorganization. A special anti-Basmachi force was created in eastern Bukhara. One infantry and two cavalry brigades, three infantry and one cavalry regiment, as well as auxiliary forces and the forces of the Bukharan People's Republic were included. In May a Central Asian bureau of the Central Committee of the Russian Communist Party was organized to coordinate the efforts of the Communist parties of Turkestan, Bukhara and Khiva. A prominent Communist leader of Georgian origin, Ordjonikidze, arrived in Bukhara from Moscow in May and sharply rebuked the hesitant policy of the Bukharan satellite government.[16] S. S. Kamenev, the commander-in-chief of the Red Army, coordinated military preparations in the area. Soviet troops soon moved against the main Basmachi forces of Ibragim-bek and Enver Pasha.

On the Basmachi side there was little agreement among the leaders. Ibragim-bek, jealous of favors shown by the Emir to Enver, split with Enver. Faizulla Maksum, another important Basmachi leader, followed the same course. As a result, Soviet troops recaptured Diushambe and further pressed the rebels. On August 4, 1922, Enver was killed in an insignificant engagement. The new commander, Selim Pasha, selected by a Basmachi conference in Kabul,[17] and approved by the Emir, was a Turk and a friend of Enver. Unrecognized by many Basmachi leaders (thereby failing to unite the movement), he committed suicide in the Piandj river. In the meantime, a Basmachi terrorist attempt on the life of Faizulla Khodzhaev, new chairman of the Bukharan Council of People's Commissars, failed on July 7, 1922.[18]

The Soviet offensive was not limited to Tajikistan. An internal struggle between Uzbek and Kirgiz units in the Fergana valley had weakened the Basmachi movement. On several occasions the Kirgiz chieftain, Muetdin, remained "neutral" during Soviet actions against Uzbek Basmachi. In November the foremost Uzbek Basmachi leader in the area, Kur-Shirmat, left Fergana and went to Afghanistan, leaving formal command to his Kirgiz rival, Muetdin. This attempt to unify the competing Basmachi groups failed. New fights began between Muetdin and the Uzbek chieftain, Israil, who was discontented by this arrangement. In January, 1922, Kur-Shirmat returned from Afghanistan and tried to unite the movement, but failed again. July found Muetdin defeated by Soviet forces, and after this the Kirgiz Basmachi groups began to surrender. Uzbek Basmachi units, left alone, were rapidly losing ground. Kur-Shirmat fled to Afghanistan. The number of Basmachi in the area fell to two thousand.[19]

Soviet authorities finally understood that military measures should be connected to political and economic concessions. On May 26, 1922, Tashkent temporarily reestablished religious *Kazi* courts in the Fergana valley and returned the lands formerly held by Moslem religious institutions (*Vakufs*). At the same time, taxes were cut in half in Fergana,[20] and food supplies were sent to the area. The liberal approach of the New Economic Policy, first introduced in summer, 1921, as well as long-awaited land and water reforms, had begun to bear fruit. Peasants, having had enough of the revolt, wanted to work.[21] In the Fergana valley alone, during the first nine months of

1923, the Basmachi lost over 3,500 men. In addition, relations between Uzbek and Kirgiz Basmachi still did not improve. The offer of amnesty attracted many. In July, S. S. Kamenev, reviewing the Soviet forces in the area, declared that the Basmachi movement in Fergana would soon be destroyed.[22] Nevertheless, he took no chances and ordered intensive use of aircraft in dealing with remaining Basmachi strongholds.[23]

After the deaths of Enver and Selim, Ibragim-bek reaffirmed his supreme position among the Basmachi in Tajikistan, but this came too late. Basmachi troops had suffered heavy losses. Their leadership, despite Ibragim-bek's supremacy, still remained divided. In the Bukharan territory the Metchi mountain stronghold was wiped out by a strong Soviet task force (March, 1923). In July the head of the Central Asian Bureau of the Central Committee of the Russian Communist Party, Ia. Rudzutak, visited Bukhara and pressed for further intensification of anti-Basmachi operations.

The Basmachi movement in the Samarkand-Bukhara area was nearing destruction. Only in the desert areas of Khorezm were the Basmachi still able to gather large forces. In January, 1924, a very strong force under Djunaid-Khan attacked Khiva, but was repulsed.[24] This was the last large-scale Basmachi operation in Central Asia.

By 1925 Tajikistan, the center of the Basmachi revolt, was in ruin. Over 200,000 inhabitants had already fled to Afghanistan, leaving two-thirds of the arable land abandoned. In relatively less-affected Uzbekistan, one-fourth of the land was abandoned.[25]

Ibragim-bek tried a comeback in 1925, but the country had been bled white and the people were too tired to continue what was obviously a hopeless resistance. The peasants wanted peace at any price. From 57 groups with 1,370 men, the Basmachi troops in Tajikistan dwindled to 29 groups with 959 men (spring, 1926).[26] The long-overdue land reform, finally conducted in Tajikistan in 1924, began to produce results favorable to the Soviet regime. A Communist Party organization was created in Tajikistan, underlining the fact of Soviet control of the area. After the 1926 campaign Soviet authorities were at last able to cut the number of troops engaged in mopping-up operations.[27] Reduced to small bands, many Basmachi took the still available opportunity of Soviet amnesty.[28] Their leaders, Ibragim-bek, Kuram-bek and others, fled to Afghanistan. By 1927 the Basmachi forces in Tajikistan were reduced even further, but some small bands were still active, and a Basmachi chieftain, Rakhman, was still operating from across the border.[29]

In 1928 even Djunaid-Khan was forced to flee to Afghanistan. In Tajikistan, Maksum, the new head of the Tajik Soviet government, was able to induce the peasants, already tired of the hopeless struggle, to return to their lands. About thirty-three thousand peasants (out of two hundred thousand refugees) returned to Tajikistan from Afghanistan.[30] Fresh Russian cavalry units crushed the remnants of Basmachi troops in the countryside.[31]

The Basmachi movement, almost dead, was revived in 1929 by the Soviet action of forcing collectivization upon reluctant peasants. Ibragim-bek himself was caught by Soviet troops in June, 1931, but remnants of Basmachi groups, often reduced to banditry, survived until 1933.[32] After years of uneven struggle, all trace of military resistance was crushed. The local native population was finally subdued and Soviet peace was established in Central Asia.

Chapter 4

Economic Life

Collectivization and Cattle Breeding

CENTRAL ASIAN ECONOMY emerged from the Revolution in a state of total chaos. In many areas the production fell to 20 per cent of the prerevolutionary level.[1] However, the liberal approach of the New Economic Policy (NEP) stimulated the recovery, despite the continuous Basmachi revolt.[2] Two agricultural reforms were carried out after the establishment of the Soviet regime. The first one consisted of confiscating lands and water rights belonging to local *bais* (landlords) and distributing them to the *dekhane* (Moslem peasants). Started in 1921, then expanded in 1925–27, this reform brought little practical result and fell short of expectations. It was, nevertheless, willingly accepted by the native peasant masses. Farmers' cooperatives, or *Koshchi* unions, organized on a voluntary basis by 1927, included 60 per cent of peasant households. They helped the rural population to buy necessary farm tools and to market their products.[3] This period of economic stabilization was interrupted in 1929 by the social and economic revolution caused by the collectivization drive. Settled peasants were pressured to join the collective farms. Nomads were forced to settle *and* to join the collective farms. The previously successful farmers' cooperatives were abandoned. An American technician, who was working in Kazakhstan at that time, reported:

When the Communist shock troops began to break up those herds and to put pressure on the nomad owners to pool their animals in so-called collective farms, the latter simply killed their animals. . . . The ex-nomads who survived this period were rounded up as the *kulaks* have been. . . . Many of them resisted dispossession; these were adjudged criminals, and sent to jail or shot.[4]

During this struggle, the animal stock of the area was decimated. Millions of head of cattle were slaughtered by the peasants and the nomads; millions more perished in the resulting chaos (see Table 1). The yield of wheat in the cultivated areas of Kazakhstan dropped from the usual 5.7–6.3 centners per hectare to 4.0 in 1931 and 4.4 in 1932.[5] "Counterrevolutionary elements," *bais*, Basmachi and other traditional black characters were charged by the authorities as causing the hardships. Scores of native Communists were removed for softness and negligence. Others were executed for "bourgeois nationalism" because of their opposition to forced collectivization. Despite all the troubles, the bulk of private farming was collectivized between 1929 and 1932, with the percentage of collectivized land increasing in Uzbekistan from 1.2 in 1928–29 to 68.1 in 1932 and 95 in 1937; in Kazakhstan

Table 1

CATTLE IN CENTRAL ASIA
(in 1,000 heads, pigs excluded)

	1929	Collectivization (1929–32)	1932–33	1960
Kazakhstan[a]	36,000	?	5,029	33,633
Central Asia proper	23,151[b]	?	9,120[c]	24,623[d]

a Compiled from *Kazakhstan*, p. 132, Vincent Monteil, "Essai sur l'Islam en URSS," *Revue des études islamiques*, Vol. XX (1952), p. 34; "Kazakhskaia SSR," *Bolshaia Sovetskaia Entsiklopediia (BSE)* 1st ed., Vol. SSSR., p. 1850, and *SSSR v Tsifrakh. Statisticheskii Sbornik* (Moscow: Gos. statisticheskoe izd., 1960), p. 157.

b *Kazakhstan*, p. 150; T. R. Ryskulov, *Kazakhstan* (Moscow: Ogiz, Sotsegiz, 1935), p. 101; "Uzbekskaia SSR," *Malaia Sovetskaia Entsiklopediia (MSE)*, 1st ed., Vol. 9, pp. 32, 106; Rakhimbaev, *op. cit.*, p. 74.

c France. Institut National de la Statistique et des Études Economiques, Études et documents, *L'Asie Sovetique* (Paris: Presses Universitaires, 1949), p. 187.

d SSSR v Tsifrakh. *loc. cit.*

from 2.7 in 1928 to 98.3 in 1935.[6] The rest of Central Asia followed.[7]

In 1942 Soviet authorities allowed former nomad cattle breeders to resume their traditional way of life, more appropriate to soil conditions in the area, but no retreat from the collective farm system was even contemplated. The preceding table gives a clear picture of the impact of collectivization upon the traditional cattle-breeding economy of non-irrigated lands of Central Asia.

Cotton and Grains

Since prerevolutionary days Central Asia has been the main cotton area of the USSR, accounting for about 90 per cent of the total production. Cotton is grown on the irrigated lands, in the valleys and oases. The heart of the cotton land is in the Fergana valley.

One of the chief accusations leveled by the Soviets against the tsarist economic policy in Central Asia was that the latter had transformed the area into "a cotton appendix of Russia" (Lenin). The British policy in Egypt was also directed at pushing cotton production at the expense of grain,[8] but as a matter of fact, the Soviet government has always followed the same policy. This can be seen from Tables 2 and 3, showing the shifts in cotton

Table 2

COTTON AND GRAINS IN UZBEKISTAN*

Area Under Cultivation (in 1,000 hectares)

Crop	1913	1938	1950	1957	1961
Cotton	423.5	917.2	955	1,347	1,446
All Cereals	1,521	1,452.7	1,371	1,010	1,019
Rice only	161	80.4	52.8	50 (1956)	

* Compiled from *BSE*, 1st ed., Vol. 55, p. 635, and Vol. SSSR, p. 1840; from *SSSR v Tsifrakh. Statisticheskii Sbornik* (Moscow: Gos. statisticheskoe izd., 1958), pp. 213, 236–237; *Narodnoe Khoziaistvo Uzbekskoi SSR. Statisticheskii Sbornik* (Tashkent, 1957), p. 77; *Ezhegodnik BSE*, 1961, p. 155; *Narodnoe Khoziaistvo SSSR v 1961 g. Statisticheskii ezhegodnik* (Moscow, 1962), pp. 324, 332.

and grain cultivation in Uzbekistan, the republic which accounts for over three-fourths of the total cotton production in Central Asia.

The increase of cotton lands was closely connected with the decrease of area occupied by grains, and especially by rice, despite the fact that rice is the major component in the local diet. This artificial shortage of rice was felt especially during the war years. Faizulla Khodhzaev, the former head of the Uzbek government, executed during the Great Purge, had to confess his opposition to the Soviet cotton policy:

> We laid the economic plans in such a way as to have less cotton, because that industrial crop more than any other was binding Uzbekistan to the Soviet Union; secondly, we planned to develop agriculture in Uzbekistan so as to extend grain farming . . . in order to be independent of Russian grain.[9]

Khodzhaev and a number of local leaders supposedly holding similar opinions were liquidated. The cotton policy won out once and for all, and the economy of Central Asia became "completely immersed into that of the country as a whole."[10]

While increasing cotton production in Central Asia at the expense of grains, Soviet planners have been strongly promoting the development of grain-producing Siberian-type black soil areas of northern Kazakhstan. Since the death of Stalin, this policy received further impetus. Hundreds of thousands of Party and Young Communist League (*Komsomol*) members were sent to farm the area, despite adverse climatic conditions (growing season: 120 to 122 days; average July temperature, over thirty degrees centigrade; average June temperature, under forty degrees centigrade).[11] Elsewhere, farming is limited to valleys and oases, while about 60 per cent of the total territory is comprised of deserts. The following table shows the development of grain and cotton production in Central Asia.

Table 3

COTTON AND GRAIN PRODUCTION
IN CENTRAL ASIA AND KAZAKHSTAN
(in 1,000 tons)*

Grains	1913	1940	1961	Percentage of Total USSR Production in 1961
Kazakhstan	2,162	2,516	14,672	10.7
Central Asia proper	1,822	1,637	1,242	0.9
Cotton				
Kazakhstan	15	94	216	4.8
Central Asia proper	646	1,864	4,029	89.1

* *SSSR v Tsifrakh v 1959 g.* (Moscow: 1960) and *ibid.* for 1961 (Moscow: 1962). The population of Kazakhstan accounted for 4.35 per cent and the population of Central Asia proper for 6.55 per cent of the total population of the USSR in 1959.

Central Asia is also rich in silk, fruit and astrakhan furs. The Uzbek republic alone is the largest Soviet producer of dried fruit, and accounts for half of Soviet silk production.

Industry

The industrial development of Central Asia is of recent origin. Prior to the October, 1917, Revolution, Central Asia was a purely agrarian and cattle-breeding area, with a few cotton-ginning and silk-spinning mills (see Chapter 1, p. 29). The Soviet five-year plans and the wartime evacuation of several large industrial enterprises into that area brought about a number of changes. Kazakhstan now produces three-fourths of all Soviet lead and two-fifths of all zinc and copper. Kirgizstan is the leading mercury producer in the USSR and Uzbekistan is third in chemical fertilizers. Largest Soviet fluorspar deposits are located north of Diushambe (Tajikistan). Rare metals are found in many areas and the important nonferrous-metals industry is growing. The area around the Uzbek capital of Tashkent is an important industrial center where agricultural machinery, chemicals and steel are produced. Oil is extracted in the Krasnovodsk area of Turkmenistan (one-half of Central Asian production) and in the Guyev and

Table 4

INDUSTRIAL OUTPUT IN CENTRAL ASIA AND KAZAKHSTAN*

	1913	1928	1940	1945	1961	Approx. Percentage of USSR Output in 1961
Steel[a] (in 1,000 tons)	—	—	11	25	630	0.9
Coal[b] (in 1,000 tons)	131	228	1,689	1,319	43,121	8.5
Oil[c] (in 1,000 tons)	260	286	1,433	1,914	9,952	6.0
Cement[d] (in 1,000 tons)	—	19	267	104	4,392	8.5
Electroenergy[e] (in million kwh)	7	42	1,310	2,578	21,168	6.5

* *SSSR v Tsifrakh v 1961 g.* (Moscow: 1962), and same for 1958. See also *Narodnoe Khoziaistvo Kazakhskoi SSR—Statisticheskii Sbornik,* Alma-Ata, 1957; *Uzbekistan za 40 let Sovetskoi vlasti. Statisticheskii Sbornik* (Tashkent, 1957).

a In 1961: 313.4 in Uzbekistan and 316.8 in Kazakhstan.

b Up to 1950's over three-fourths in Kirgizstan; 1961: Kazakhstan, 34,579.

c In 1913, half in Turkmenistan and half in Kazakhstan. Turkmen oil production at standstill in 1928; in 1940's divided between Kazakhstan, Turkmenistan and Uzbekistan (in the order of importance); in 1961, Turkmenistan, 6,100; Kazakhstan, 1,700; Uzbekistan, 1,705.

d Up to the 1950's exclusively Uzbekistan. In 1961, Kazakhstan, 2,591; Uzbekistan, 1,199.

e In the 1940's, divided between Kazakhstan and Uzbekistan, with small output elsewhere. In 1961, Kazakhstan, 11,524; Uzbekistan, 6,750. Despite this development only 35 per cent of collective farms in Uzbekistan had electricity in 1959 (15 in 1950).

Aktiubinsk areas of Kazakhstan, and coal is mined in Karaganda and the Ekibastuz areas of Kazakhstan, and in Kirgizstan. The preceding table shows the development of the main branches of Central Asian industry.

The War Effort (Uzbekistan during World War II)

During World War II, Central Asia was far enough from the front to enjoy immunity even from air attacks. The war conditions, nevertheless, exercised a dominant, albeit indirect, influence on all the aspects of life in the area.

According to Soviet sources, Uzbekistan alone already had 1,445 large-scale industrial enterprises in 1940. During the war years 280 new enterprises went into service, including such industrial giants as the second and third sections of the Chirchik Nitrogen-Fertilizer works, the first open-hearth furnace of the Uzbek Iron and Steel Works, the Uzbek Metallurgical Works, large hydroelectric stations, chemical and metal-working plants, canneries, sugar refineries, spinning and weaving factories, silk-weaving and -spinning mills. Over one hundred large enterprises were transferred from European Russia. Thus the machine-building Engels factory was evacuated from Leningrad; *Elektrostanok, Elektrokabel* and *Podyemnik* from Moscow; *Rostselmash* from Rostov and a number of other large factories from other cities. As a result of these transfers and of new local constructions, the structure of the Uzbek industry was radically transformed, with heavy industry taking the main share of the country's industrial output (48.5 per cent in 1943 as against 13.3 per cent in 1940).[12]

Hundreds of thousands of refugees poured into the area. Some came by themselves, escaping the German advance. Others, like the Poles, were released from Siberian camps. Most of the newcomers were absorbed by urban areas. As a result, many cities doubled their population. Samarkand, a city of 150,000 people, absorbed an additional 150,000. Tashkent doubled its population, increasing from 585,000 in 1939 to about 1,000,000 in 1944.[13] Housing and sanitary conditions, already poor in peacetime, became worse. Epidemics spread through the crowded, undernourished population. The local authorities were caught among the economic imperatives of the war economy, the overflow of refugees, the runaway inflation, the shortage of manpower and a number of secondary effects resulting from the over-all situation. Top priority production goals were pushed ahead regardless of sacrifice involved, while the production of less essential items was neglected or set aside. As a result, between 1940 and 1945 the over-all output of Uzbek industry remained almost static.

Mobilization deprived Central Asia of an adequate labor force. To remedy the situation, consumer goods and other "peacetime industries" started to lay off some of their employees.[14] Moscow issued decrees allowing local authorities to relocate such employees whenever necessary. All men between the ages of sixteen and fifty-five and all women between the ages of sixteen and forty-five became subject to labor draft. Some of the large factories established a twelve-hour working day, which was named "optimum labor day." Some other factories went on a seven-day working week. Between 1940 and 1943 the number of industrial workers in Uzbekistan increased from 129,100 to 187,200, but the percentage of women among them rose from 34.1 to 63.5.[15] This means that the number of male workers decreased by over 15 per cent, with women replacing men in the large majority of factory jobs. The evacuated factories were given about 100,000 local workers, leaving the existing industries with only 87,000 workers in 1943, that is, with two-thirds of their prewar personnel.

The industrial development of the capital city of Tashkent and its vicinity was vigorously pushed ahead (especially on account of large, evacuated enterprises producing war needs), but industrial activity in all the other regions of Uzbekistan suffered serious setbacks and by 1945 fell to between one-half and three-quarters of the prewar level.[16] In the Samarkand region the metallurgical industry increased three and one-half times, but the food and the textile industries had fallen by half, and the over-all industrial activity went down by one-quarter.[17] Prior to the war Central Asia (Kazakhstan excepted) was importing grain and various consumer goods from Russia. During the war it was forced to rely entirely on its own food production. This was made especially difficult because of the traditional emphasis placed by the Soviet government upon the increase of cotton production in that area at the expense of food production. During the war years, however, the very course of events compelled Soviet authorities to do their best in order to make Uzbekistan fully independent of Russian and Siberian grain.[18] More than that, Uzbekistan had to feed the newly arrived refugee masses and, in addition, to fulfill increasing food-delivery quotas imposed by Moscow.[19] To cope with this problem, it was decided to increase the amount of land under grain cultivation in Uzbekistan by 500,000 hectares and to increase the grain production two and one-half times or even threefold.[20] These decisions remained, however, on paper, while the production of foodstuffs went down; between 1940 and 1945 the production of vegetable oils fell from 142,000 tons to 41,000; of wine, from 1,928,000 decaliters to 634,000; of pastry, from 13,000 tons to 4,900. Probably meat and milk production also fell, since five years after the war ended (in 1950) it stood at two-thirds of the 1940 level. The absence of grain and vegetable statistics and the decrease of lands under grain and vegetable cultivation suggest an even worse picture.[21]

The precarious farming situation was made worse by the large-scale mobilization of farmers for the construction of big hydroelectric dams. The giant Farkhad hydroelectric works alone employed 70,000 collective farmers in February, 1943.[22]

Food and consumer-goods shortages led to inflation. In 1942, the black-market price of bread skyrocketed to approximately fifty rubles per pound, as against the official price of forty kopecks. The cost of vegetables increased almost fifty times. Meat and butter went up twenty times, clothing ten to twenty. An average employee's monthly wage, frozen at the prewar level, was barely sufficient to cover a few days of substandard existence. State grocery prices were also frozen, but nothing was sold without a ration card, and seldom was anything but limited quantities of bread made available this way. The average citizen had to buy his food on the collective-farm market and his clothing on the black market. The only possible way to survive was to make money in addition to the official salary. For the large majority of workers and employees this could be done only through appropriation of state property, black marketing, or graft.

Factory directors and office managers were forced to let workers "take" some of the goods produced or distributed by the enterprise, because the workers could not possibly exist or produce on their meager salaries alone. The degree of appropriation depended upon individual enterprise, local conditions and personal position. Craftsmen in cooperative enterprises, truck drivers, food salesmen, or heads of warehouses were in relatively good money-making positions. Bookkeepers, accountants and various inspectors were usually able to demand their share. Managers and directors of various enterprises, factories, offices, and cooperatives were still in the best spot: they were able to make more money than anybody else, and, in addition, had access to special stores reserved for the privileged Party economic elite. Workers in defense factories were also supplied from their own special stores, but in a much more limited way than the privileged group. Factory and office workers in all other enterprises were worse off; they were barely able to keep themselves alive. Since practically every employee was guilty of acts against the law, the state was in a position to bring to court almost anyone and for "just cause."

The collective farmers seemed to be the only beneficiaries of the inflation. They were busy selling the products of their private plots, as well as those received on payment for their labor, at a high price. Collective farm chairmen and other rural dignitaries prospered. One could see them on the main streets of some local villages wearing odd European clothes traded by Polish or Russian refugees. But for rank-and-file members of collective farms, this rather unusual prosperity did not last too long. Many among them were soon mobilized into the army, the labor front or the many hydroelectric works in progress. Those remaining, mostly women, children and older men, had to work harder than ever and for less compensation. Two years after the end of the war (December, 1947) old rubles were exchanged for new ones at the rate of ten to one, depriving the collective farmers of the gains made during the inflation.

Chapter 5

The Settlers

SOVIET CENTRAL ASIA is roughly one-half of the United States in area. At the time of the Revolution, it contained over two million people of Slavic stock and about twelve million natives (mostly Sunni Moslems), divided into a number of groups: Uzbeks, Kazakhs, Kirgizes, Turkmen, Tajiks, Kara-Kalpaks, Uigurs, Kurama, Dungans, Sart-Kalmuks, Djemshids, Chasara, Bukhara Jews, Mountain Iranian tribes and others. Among these indigenous groups only the first five were numerically important: the Uzbeks and Kazakhs numbered over three and a half million each, while the Tajiks, Kirgizes and Turkmen were each under a million. The Tajiks belong to the Iranian ethnic group. The other four belong to the Turkic, and speak languages related to Turkish.

The Slavic population was concentrated mostly in three areas: north of the Steppe Region bordering on Siberia, in the black-soil lands of the Semirechye and in the Tashkent area. About half of the settlers were relative newcomers, having arrived after 1906, following Stolypin's "virgin land program."[1]

After the October Revolution and during the early 1920's, Russian colonization of Central Asia was temporarily arrested. After 1928, however, Slavic (mostly Russian and Ukrainian) colonization was resumed, and, by 1936, 1,700,000 new settlers had moved into the area: 786,000 into Uzbekistan; 156,000 into Turkmenistan; 290,000 into Kirgizstan; 202,000 into Tajikistan (Kazakhstan not accounted for).[2] By 1939, the Slavs consti-

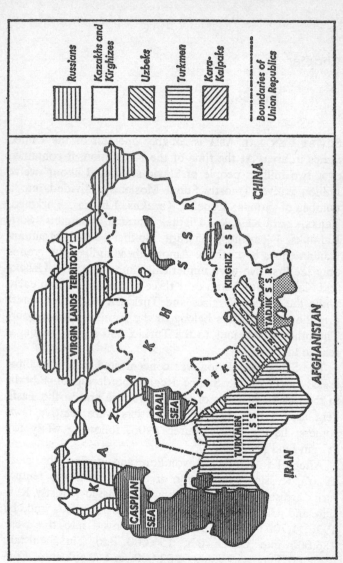

The (Rural) Population of Central Asia

tuted half of the population of the main city of the area, Tashkent.[3] Although many newcomers were deportees exiled to Central Asia as persons politically or socially dangerous to the Soviet regime due to their national origin, they involuntarily found themselves in the role of promoters of Soviet Russia's colonial policy in Central Asia. The same was true for non-Russian newcomers, since many natives failed to make a distinction between the Russians and the other national groups of European origin. The latter, on the other hand, under the impact of local conditions, soon developed a kind of common "European solidarity" with the Russians vis-à-vis the natives.

The German invasion of Russia in 1941 brought another wave of newcomers: employees of evacuated enterprises and their families, refugees from German-occupied territories, and Polish citizens released from Soviet camps in Siberia.[4]

The majority of the newcomers returned to their homelands after the war; those who stayed again increased the proportion of non-natives in all the republics of Soviet Central Asia. As a result of industrialization, urbanization and wartime population movements, some previously native cities became heavily Russified. To give an example from recent data, in the city of Samarkand, Uzbeks and Tajiks together account for only 39.5 per cent of the population, while Russians, Ukrainians and Byelorussians account for 36.9 per cent. Koreans constitute 1.4 per cent; others (probably mostly Russian and Bukhara Jews, Armenians, Tatars, Volga Germans, etc.) 22.2 per cent.[5] The mayor of Samarkand, Shakirov, in an interview with Adlai Stevenson during his 1958 tour of Russia, felt the necessity to cover up the existing situation by stating that Russians account for only 10 or 12 per cent of the city's population.[6]

New deportations of so-called "politically unreliable"

persons and national groups continued during and immediately after the war. These included Volga Germans, Crimean Tatars, Chechens, inhabitants of the Baltic states and others. Khrushchev's "virgin land program" of the mid-1950's resulted in the latest wave of over 600,000 Russian, Ukrainian, Byelorussian and Latvian settlers. The newcomers have been directed to the black-soil areas of Northern and Southern Kazakhstan.[7] In addition to economic motives stressed by the Soviet authorities, the possible desire to populate the area before the expected Chinese demographic explosion of the end of this century may have played a role. The operation was conducted according to the traditional Russian policy of settlement by a "stream which penetrates and covers the regions which are most thinly inhabited."[8]

From the demographic viewpoint, the consecutive waves of voluntary and involuntary colonization have brought about an important change in the original national composition of the population in Central Asia and Kazakhstan. The total number of people of European origin (Russians, Ukrainians, Byelorussians, Germans, Jews and others) has exceeded that of any single indigenous national group in that area. Proportionate to native populations, Europeans are more numerous in Soviet Central Asia and Kazakhstan than, for example, in the Union of South Africa or Algeria. The percentage of Europeans in the total population (1959 census) is 65 per cent in Kazakhstan and approximately 25 per cent in Soviet Central Asia. In the Union of South Africa, on the other hand, the percentage of people of European origin amounts to only 21 per cent and in Algeria (before independence) to only 14 per cent. Russian settlement of Central Asia and of Kazakhstan is so rapid that many experts in the field grossly underestimate its extent.[9]

Table 5 is based on a critical analysis of the 1926,

1939 and 1959 Soviet censuses. Soviet Moslem dignitaries, for their part, feel uneasy over the extent of Russian settlement in Central Asia. Thus Mansur Mirza-Akhmedov, the 1958 prime minister of Uzbekistan, declared to Adlai Stevenson in Tashkent that Russians (and other Slavs) constitute only 11 per cent of the population of Uzbekistan, a figure absolutely unrealistic even if compared to the 1939 Soviet statistics.

Table 5

PERCENTAGE OF EUROPEANS IN CENTRAL ASIA

	1926	1939	1959
Kazakhstan	34.9[a]	47 [f]	64.9[k]
Uzbekistan	5.6[b]	17.8[g]	18.4[l]
Turkmenistan	7.5[c]	18.7[h]	24.2[m]
Kirgizstan	18.89[d]	34 [i]	43.8[n]
Tajikistan	0.7[e]	10.3[j]	19.1[o]

[a] Caroe (Sir Olaf Kirkpatrick), *Soviet Empire. The Turcs of Central Asia and Stalinism* (London: Macmillan and Co., 1953); p. 166.

[b] "Uzbekskaia SSR" (*MSE*), 1st ed., Vol. IX, p. 105.

[c] "Turkmenskaia SSSR," *ibid.*, p. 31.

[d] T. R. Ryskulov, *Kirgizstan* (Moscow, 1935), p. 11.

[e] T. R. Rakhimbaev, *Tadzhikistan* (Moscow: Sotsegiz, 1936), p. 27.

[f] *Ibid.*, pp. 168–170, and Akademiia Nauk SSSR, Institut Geografii, *Kazakhskaia SSSR; ekonomiko-geograficheskaia kharakteristika* (Moscow: Geografgiz, 1957), p. 130. It indicates that in 1939 Kazakhs accounted for only 57 per cent of the population of their republic, Russians and Ukrainians for 33 per cent, Uzbeks 3 per cent, others (natives and non-natives) 7 per cent. It also states that the percentage of Kazakhs was much smaller because of the influx of newcomers. In some regions (Karaganda) it reached the low point of 30 per cent (p. 131). Another indication is that 66 per cent of the school-age children attended Russian schools and only 34 per cent attended native schools (p. 146).

[g] My own calculation. *BSE*, 2nd ed., Vol. XLIV, p. 11, fixes the percentage of Russians at 11.6 and that of Ukrainians, European and Asiatic Jews, Uigurs and Gypsies together at 6.7. The first two groups (Ukrainians and Russian Jews) account for at least two-thirds of the 6.7 per cent.

[h] Z. G. Freikin, *Turkmenskaia SSR* (Moscow, Geografgiz, 1954), p. 84, and *BSE*, 2nd ed., Vol. XLIII, p. 449.

The extent of Russian colonization in Central Asia has been determined by a number of powerful factors:

1. While the colonial possessions of other European powers were geographically separated from their mother country, Russian Central Asia and Kazakhstan are contiguous to Great Russia itself.

2. The growing industry of Central Asia demanded more skilled labor than the area could supply.[10]

3. The entire area, especially Kazakhstan and Turkmenistan, is underpopulated and can absorb millions of settlers. According to recent German estimates, Central Asia and Southern Kazakhstan (that is, the area of old Turkestan) have space for a maximum of 100,000,000 people, probably for 45,000,000 and at least for 20,000,000. Corresponding estimates for Northern Kazakhstan alone are 57,500,000; 27,500,000; and 10,000,000.[11] Despite all the Soviet efforts to populate the area, even the minimum level figures have yet to be reached.

4. The combination of natural increase and immigra-

---

i My own estimate. "Kirgizy," *BSE*, 2nd ed., Vol. XXI, p. 102, gives the percentage of Kirgizes in their republic as 51.7.

j *Ibid.*, Vol. XLI, 2nd ed., p. 471.

k "Ob urovne obrazovaniia, natsionalnom sostave i vozrastnoi strukture naseleniia SSSR po dannym Vsesoiuznoi perepisi naseleniia 1959 goda"; *Pravda*, February 4, 1960, gives the following figures: Russians—42.7 per cent, Ukrainians—8.2 per cent, Byelorussians—1.2 per cent, Poles—0.6 per cent. Nonlisted are 12.2 per cent who can be added to the non-native group, since native groups are listed down to the Dungans (0.1 per cent). Among the nonlisted 12.2 per cent there is a large number of Germans, but also Latvians, Jews and many others. Tatars and Koreans are not included among non-natives in this table. Same pattern applies to all the 1959 figures below.

l *Ibid.* gives the following figures: Russians—13.6 per cent, Ukrainians—1.1 per cent, Jews—1.2 per cent. Nonlisted are 3.1 per cent. Only half of the Jews are counted as non-natives, since there are a number of native Bukhara Jews in Uzbekistan.

m *Ibid.* Russians—17.3 per cent, Ukrainians—1.4 per cent, Armenians—1.3 per cent. Nonlisted are 4.2 per cent.

n *Ibid.* Russians—30.2 per cent, Ukrainians—6.6 per cent. Nonlisted are 7.0 per cent.

o *Ibid.* Russians—13.3 per cent, Ukrainians—1.4 per cent. Nonlisted are 4.4 per cent.

tion of Russians and of other Europeans exceeded, until the end of World War II, the increase of the native population in Central Asia. Due to the recent "virgin land program" this is still the case in Kazakhstan. It may not be the case, however, in Central Asia itself, where the native birth rate is said to have increased, and Russian immigration decreased, in the 1950's.

5. Since the beginning of Russian conquest, Central Asia has been used as a land of exile for various "politically unreliable" persons, starting with the Polish rebels of the 1860's.

The large European population of Central Asia plays a decisive role in the political, cultural and economic life of the area. In the hypothetical case of a nationalist struggle for independence from Russia, the Russian settlers may not react too differently from their French-Algerian counterparts. As told by a Russian settler to a French correspondent in Uzbekistan, "Change the terminology and you will find the same problem you are dealing with in North Africa."[12]

The attempts made by some native Communist leaders to stop the waves of Russian migration have been unsuccessful. Nasrattulah Maksum, president of the Tajik Supreme Soviet, who tried to oppose Russian colonization in Tajikistan, was liquidated in 1933. Similar attempts by Kazakh Communists Sultanbekov, Dulatov and Sasvokasov also ended in failure.[13]

The influx of Russian settlers had a decisive bearing on the economic development of Central Asia. Before the large-scale Russian immigration, the area was faced with several problems peculiar to underdeveloped areas in general: the presence of a large Moslem population of Turkic stock hostile to, or at least suspicious of, Russia and Russians in general; the presence of large numbers of nomads reluctant to change their customary way of life; lack of industry and, consequently, of a native proletariat;

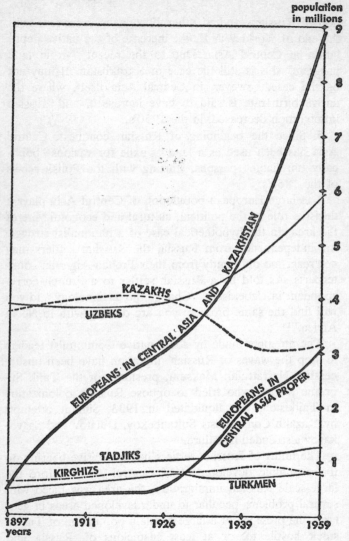

population
in millions

9

8

7

6

5

KAZAKHSTAN

KA'ZAKHS

UZBEKS

4

EUROPEANS IN CENTRAL ASIA AND KAZAKHSTAN

3

EUROPEANS IN CENTRAL ASIA PROPER

2

TADJIKS

1

KIRGHIZS

TURKMEN

1897
years

1911

1926

1939

1959

Growth of Population According to Nationalities: Central Asia
and Kazakhstan (1897, 1911, 1926, 1939, 1959 censuses)

extreme scarcity of local technicians and white-collar workers; extreme scarcity of even fairly educated natives.

The tremendous industrial development of Central Asia during the years of the Soviet regime has transformed the entire economy and created a large urban working class. The majority of nonagricultural employees in Central Asia is still, however, non-native, since the growth of the native working class has not matched the growth of industry. Of the nonagricultural cadres in Central Asia, non-natives are in the majority among managers and technicians in industry and mining, white-collar workers, skilled and semi-skilled labor. Natives, on the other hand, predominate as managers of consumer-goods enterprises and cooperatives, as craftsmen in local industries and as unskilled laborers.

Despite Soviet efforts to develop native technical cadres, by 1956 Uzbeks accounted for only 10 per cent of the engineers, 11 per cent of the doctors and 12 per cent of the technicians in their own republic.[14] Recent Soviet statistics corroborate these evaluations. This "division of labor" according to national lines is confirmed by many other sources. One study evaluates the native urban labor force in Uzbekistan at one-third of the total: 300,000 out of 900,000 in 1956.[15] A similar division of the labor force existed at that time in Kazakhstan. Another study considers that the percentage of native workers in Uzbek industry, while rising in the 1920's, remained at a steady 50 per cent of the total from the beginning of the 1930's until the start of World War II. It evaluates the percentage of native workers in industry as follows:*

1924–26	29 %
1928	44.3%
1930	50 %
1938	about 50 %

* Franck A. Ecker, *Transition in Asia.* Unpublished Ph.D. dissertation, University of Michigan, 1954, p. 40.

In the 1940's the natives were still in a minority among industrial workers. *Pravda Vostoka* gives a number of examples in support of this assertion. A 1941 article states that Uzbeks accounted for only 18 per cent of the technical personnel in thirty-six large enterprises selected from all over the Republic.[16] Another article states that in the few large industrial enterprises listed below, the percentage of natives was as follows: *Uzbektekstilmash* factory in Tashkent, 14.5; Ministry of Food Industry enterprises all over Uzbekistan, 30; Kaganovich factory in Tashkent, 14.1; Margelan Silk Combine, 35.[17]

Another article describing the situation at one of the most important factories in Uzbekistan, the *Podyemnik* factory, states that no natives were trained for foremen's jobs in 1946 and that out of sixty workers trained as fitters, turners and turret-lathe operators, only six were natives. The total number of skilled native workers at this factory dropped from eighty-nine in the beginning of 1945 to fifty-six in September, 1946, and of unskilled workers, from thirty-six to ten.[18] The continuation of such a state of affairs was officially confirmed in the resolutions of the Eleventh (1952) and Twelfth (1954) Party Congresses in Uzbekistan.[19] The strong dislike by Central Asian Moslems of factory work is often privately mentioned as a major cause for such a state of affairs.

The reliance of Uzbekistan upon the Russian labor force is well illustrated by the fact that the number of industrial workers in Uzbekistan, which increased from 129,100 in 1940 to 187,200 in 1943 after the influx of refugees, fell back to 145,600 in 1945 when a number of refugees were re-evacuated to their original location.[20] In 1914, 70 per cent of the industrial workers in Turkestan were natives, a higher proportion than at any time thereafter.[21]

Chapter 6

Cultural Policy

Linguistic Policy

NOT ONLY WERE large parts of the territory of Soviet Central Asia colonized by Slavic settlers, but local Turkic languages were not left alone either. The alphabets of Soviet Central Asia have been changed twice by the Soviet regime. At first the modified Arabic alphabet, in use since 1922, was discarded in favor of the Latin alphabet; then the Latin alphabet was dropped and replaced by the Cyrillic alphabet. The Soviet regime justified the first reform on the grounds that the Arabic alphabet, even in its modified (phonetic) version, was too difficult to learn and was too easily identified with what they called "the reactionary philosophy" of Islam. The Latin alphabet, on the other hand, being universal, would more effectively combat illiteracy, they claimed. It would, moreover, facilitate the study of Central Asian languages as well as the translation of foreign books into these languages. They also probably assumed that by adopting the Latin alphabet they could more easily control publications printed in local languages[1] and create a barrier between the new national literatures of Central Asian Republics and their common Chagatai source.[2] (Chagatai is the medieval literary language of all the Turkic peoples of Central Asia.)

Prior to 1926 the change to the Latin alphabet was conducted by persuasion only. In 1926 the principle of reform was adopted by the Turkological Congress in Baku. Subsequently, the Latin alphabet and a unified mode of transcription were implanted in most regions formerly using the Arabic script, but not until 1935 did the implantation become complete.[3]

The second reform, introduction of the Cyrillic (Russian) alphabet, began in 1935, but made no serious progress until 1939. The Soviets strongly defended this new reform. They pointed out that the Latin alphabet was useful in conquering illiteracy, but that the Cyrillic was better adapted for the transcription of Turkic sounds because it contained more letters than the Latin. There are, for example, thirty-eight sounds in the Uzbek languages and thirty-two letters in the Cyrillic alphabet, but only twenty-six letters in the Latin alphabet. They claimed that the Cyrillic alphabet would facilitate both the penetration of national tongues by the Russian language and the study of the Russian language by the natives. As explained by a Soviet linguist in 1952:

One of the most important cultural acquisitions of the peoples of the USSR . . . is the development of alphabets and systems of writing for the languages of the [minority] peoples on the basis of the Russian character. . . . The adoption of the Russian script by most of the languages has not only contributed to their development, but has been of notable assistance to the various nationalities of the Soviet Union in their successful mastery of the Russian language and in the assimilation of Russian Culture.[4]

These expectations were fulfilled. According to Western studies, the percentage of words of Russian (or Russified French) origin in the Uzbek language rose from 2 per cent in 1923 to 15 per cent in 1940. During the same time the percentage of words of Arabic or Persian origin used in the Uzbek language fell from 37 to 25.[5] A large number of Russian loan words, which entered the Uzbek language (as well as the other languages of Central Asia), are technical and political terms or modern Soviet and international abbreviations and expressions.[6] They usually maintain their original Russian transcription, but acquire an Uzbek ending when appropriate. In the 1950's, however, Uzbek endings were often dropped, and loan words appeared in the original transcription (example: the plural of *kommunist* became *kommunisty*, with a Russian plural ending, instead of *kommunistlar*). At the same time a number of existing terms of Turkic origin have been replaced by Russian ones.[7] Russian words like *obed, obida* and *obzor* entered the Uzbek language in their Russian phonetical form—*abed, abida* and *abzor*—taking the place of equivalent Turkic words.[8] (Fortunately enough, a trend toward purging of unnecessary Russian loan words from Turkic languages seems to be developing lately as a by-product of the process of liberalization of the Soviet life.) Simultaneously, the uniformity in the writing of the Turkic languages of the USSR was broken by the modification of the official Uzbek literary language. The dialect of the town of Turkestan (Kazakh SSR) was replaced in 1937 as official Uzbek literary language by the urban dialect of Tashkent, less intelligible to other Turkic peoples of the area.[9]

Whereas the first reform of the alphabet seems to have been motivated by both political and practical factors, the second appears to have been caused primarily by political considerations. It was probably felt by Moscow that the introduction of the Russian alphabet in Central Asia would recreate a cultural barrier between the Turkic subjects of Russia and Turkey, who, following the first Soviet reform, also adopted the Latin script. On the other hand, it would consolidate the cultural unity between Russia proper and her Central Asian possessions. Moreover, the introduction of the Cyrillic alphabet coincided with the denunciation of the theory of the Soviet historian Pokrovsky, condemning as an "absolute evil" any colonization, whether western or Russian.

The adoption of the Russian alphabet made obsolete millions of books already printed in Latin characters and drove thousands of natives back to semiliteracy. At the same time it enhanced the prestige of the Russian language, which according to the Soviet point of view, was to become "the second mother tongue of the non-Russian intelligentsia, . . . the language of international intercourse between various national groups of the Union."[10] As proudly stated by Soviet linguists:

> The great Russian language nourishes and enriches the languages of all our peoples, giving them its strength and force, its beauty and flexibility, its wealth and diversity.
> The enrichment of the vocabulary of the languages of all the peoples of the USSR by increasingly borrowing from Russian became a rule in their development.[11]

Not only are the Russian people to be recognized as the leading and guiding force in the country, but the Russian language is assigned a position superior to that of all other languages spoken in the Soviet Union, and future Communist nations of the USSR are envisaged as merging into one culture with one common language, Russian.

> The merging of nations in the future, the withering away and the replacement of [their] national tongues by a common language—all this will take place as a result of the flourishing of the Communist nations.
> . . . Russian is becoming more and more the common language for all the socialist nations of the USSR.[12]

The above was written in 1957 and not in the days of Stalin. It is hard to determine how much importance should be attached to these kinds of statements. On one hand, one is tempted to dismiss them altogether, along with similar Soviet dead claims about future "withering away" of state apparatus under Communism. On the other hand, such claims reinforce the position of "dogmatists" (or Stalinists) who are opposed to further liberalization of Soviet society.

Policy of Cultural Assimilation

The importance of the Russian physical and linguistic penetration should not, however, overshadow the importance of the process of cultural assimilation that is going on in that area. As seen by an American author:

> In the Soviet cultural amalgam which has emerged, Russian culture is the dominant element and to a certain extent the cultures of the ethnic minorities have been Russified. However, this process of Russification has not been the heart of the Soviet approach. National minorities have been assimilated not so much to a culture Russian in form, as Soviet in content.[13]

According to another study, however,

> . . . In many concepts, such as "Soviet culture" or "Soviet superiority," the epithet "Soviet" became a mere identification for "Russian."[14]

According to A. Bennigsen, an authority in this field, the policy of cultural Sovietization emphasizes four major themes:

1. The Moslem peoples of Central Asia are ethnically different from their Turkic and Iranian neighbors. Their common linguistic roots do not imply any cultural identity.

2. The peoples living within the territory of today's Soviet Central Asia have always felt a mutual solidarity and aspired to form one big family headed by their "big brother," the Great Russian people.

3. The national culture of the peoples of Soviet Central Asia has developed independently from outside sources and is strictly autonomous and regional. Tajik civilization, for example, is said to be of Bactrian, not Persian, origin.[15]

4. The national culture of the Central Asian peoples is superior to that of the Turkic and Iranian peoples outside the USSR, because Soviet Moslems live under the socialist regime, while foreign Moslems live under feudal or colonial oppression. It is superior also because of the supposedly richer cultural tradition of the peoples of Soviet Central Asia. In order to prove the second point, Soviet writers and historians in the early 1950's put forth exclusive claims on a number of Turkic and Iranian classical writers and scientists of the past who are part of the common cultural heritage of the entire area. Thus Ibn-Sina, Ferdawsi and Omar Khayyám were declared Tajiks, Saadi and Hafiz,—"spiritually Tajiks," in the sense of being different from other non-Tajik Iranians. (Some recent theories consider these claims to be motivated by Tajik attempts to preserve their own national-cultural identification, by stressing their rich Iranian cultural and linguistic background.) Emperor Babur (the first of the Great Moguls) was declared Uzbek. The *Avesta* of Zoroaster has been claimed simultaneously by Azerbaijan, Tajikistan and Uzbekistan; some Turkic writers have been claimed by each of the four Turkic-speaking republics of Central Asia.[16] Ali Sher Nevai became an exclusively Uzbek writer, and the Old Chagatai literature common to most of the Turkic peoples became just "Old Uzbek literature."

According to the views of émigrés from Turkestan, the official Soviet cultural policy has never been accepted by the Moslems of Central Asia. They, on the contrary, are said to lack solidarity with the Russians and to have a religious, linguistic and ethnic identification with their Moslem neighbors in Turkey and Iran.[17]

The Soviet regime, from the very beginning, adopted a position favorable to Islam's equalitarian principles, but has always been hostile to its allegedly "reactionary" social content.[18] Campaigns against Islam have been part of a permanent struggle conducted by the Soviets against all religious faiths. Considerations of local political opportunism have not been disregarded, however, and the religious issue has not always been pressed with the same determination. Religious toleration existed from 1917 to 1920 and, in somewhat curtailed form, lasted until 1928. The beginning of collectivization was accompanied by strong antireligious activity, which lasted through the purges of the 1930's. The extent of Soviet measures is also reflected in the reduction of the number of mosques in the USSR from 26,279 in 1912 to 1,312 in 1942.[19] From 1938 to 1947 antireligious activity underwent visible relaxation. This was especially true after the German invasion, when atheistic propaganda was, in its turn, curtailed for fear of its possible ill effects upon the war effort.[20] The partial survival of Islam, like that of the Russian Orthodox belief, was due to the strength of religious feelings among the common people, not to the good will of the regime. Various views are held regarding the degree of Islam's survival in Central Asia. A Pakistani traveler observes that "Islam is not fully dead yet, but appears to be in its last throes."[21]

. . . although at a first superficial glance it seems that Islam is excluded from Turkistan life . . . the Bolsheviks did not succeed in eradicating Islam. They only managed to banish the Islamic public religious worship in Mosques, that's all.

Islam as a religion, as a conception of the world, as a particular way of life remained almost untouched not only in its believers' souls, but also in the living practice.[22]

Caroe, an Englishman, sees it as occupying a position somewhere between these two opposing views:

. . . under Bolshevik pressure, religious institutions have forever lost their old meaning and force in Turkestan. . . . Yet Islam, cleaned of its theocratic accretions, lives as a spiritual possession in the hearts of the people. . . . In fact, Islam became the spiritual core of the nationalist political creed.[23]

Unable to resist Soviet Russian political and economic pressure, the natives have at least tried to preserve their cultural heritage. Moscow, however, has persisted in forcing upon them the famous Stalin principle of "culture, national in form and socialist in content." The degree of pressure and the attitude toward the local past and traditions have varied, however, from one period to another. During Stalin's rule the following variation was displayed by the Soviet authorities in their attitude toward the national cultures of Turkestan.

Prior to the middle 1930's the Pokrovsky theory of "absolute evil," which was then in force, condemned all colonial conquests, no matter whether English, French or tsarist Russian, and glorified all national-liberation movements against Great Russian oppression. In accordance with this theory, Turkestan's prerevolutionary struggle against tsarist colonization was officially lauded as part of the general revolutionary movement of the peoples of Russia. Native Communists who supported this point of view (Khodzhaev, Ikramov, Ryskulov, and their friends) were dominant in the cultural field. This period ended with their liquidation in the purges of the late 1930's, during which prominent Turkestani literary figures such as Cholpan, Fitrat, Kadyri, Elbek, Dzhumabay and Tynystan perished, among others. It coincided with the final condemnation of the historical school of Pokrovsky on August 28, 1937.

During the next period, between 1937 and the end of the 1940's, a new historical theory had been established: that of "lesser evil." According to the new theory, Russian conquests, although colonial, were lesser calamities than Turkish, Iranian or British domination. Nationalist struggle against the tsarist regime was still being lauded, but a "chauvinistic" (i.e., nationalist) outlook on its own national past was no longer tolerated from native historians.

During the war against Germany, when Soviet victory depended upon the strong fighting spirit and patriotism of the Russian people, the "big brother" role of Russia in respect to other nationalities of the USSR began to receive strong emphasis. After the war the situation did not change.

In 1951 the "lesser evil" theory received its final seal of approval from the official mouthpiece of Soviet historical science, Mme. Nechkina,[24] and was gradually drawn closer to the newest Soviet historical theory of "absolute good." The new approach was originated by the end of World War II and was encouraged by A. A. Zhdanov, the postwar Soviet arbiter of literature and art. According to the new line, the national struggle against tsarist colonization was condemned, while the virtues of union with Russia were extolled. The progressive character of tsarist colonization which carried along "the more advanced Russian culture" was stressed.[25] Kazakh historians were reminded that their native chieftains, in opposing tsarist Russian colonization, had not been patriots, but "reactionary feudals." In 1950 Shamil, the famous Caucasian Moslem nationalist leader of the nineteenth century (quoted as a "great democrat" by Marx), received a similar label.[26] The Kirgiz national epic *Manas,* pride of Soviet Kirgizstan but untimely in being anti-Chinese, was suddenly condemned as "Pan-Islamic" and "feudal" and its stunned defenders chastised[27] (this stand was recently reversed). *Alpamysh,* a part of Uzbek literary heritage, the heroic Turkestani epic describing the struggle of Turkestani Moslems against the infidel Kalmuks, was condemned in 1952 as a work inspired by Moslem fanaticism and chauvinism.[28] Popular Moslem legends suffered the same treatment. According to the Soviet custom of "self-criticism," native scholars were compelled to condemn their own previously held views and to adjust their "new opinions" accordingly.[29] Some refused to comply, but they were reduced to silence after the 1951–1952 purge of the Caucasian and Kazakh intellectuals and the faculties of Samarkand and Stalinabad Universities. The theory of "absolute good" finally triumphed.[30]

Following the new line, the conception, for example, of Kazakhstan's history was reduced, according to Walter Kolarz, a British specialist in this field, to four cut-and-dried formulae to which Kazakh writers were forced to subscribe:

The union of Kazakhstan with Russia was an aim which had been pursued by the most prominent and farsighted rulers of the Kazakh people since the end of the sixteenth century.

The union of Kazakhstan with Russia had prevented the enslavement of the Kazakhs by the "barbarian states of the Orient" and brought them into close contact with a country "incomparably more civilized" than all their Asiatic neighbors.

The annexation of Kazakhstan by Russia ended the partition of the country between China, Russia and Kokand and had opened the way to more progressive forms of economy.

All through their history the Kazakhs had never possessed a genuine well-organized state, only loosely connected semi-state organizations. The Soviet Regime had enabled Kazakhs to have a real state of their own—the Kazakh SSR.[31]

Similar positions were taken in regard to the history of Uzbekistan, Tajikistan and of other republics of Soviet Central Asia.[32] ". . . Annexation to Russia provided the Central Asian nations with the opportunity of participating in the leading culture of the Russian nation . . . ," wrote a Soviet author in 1953.[33] Tsarist Russian conquest was presented as a positive event, since it was a way of getting under the protection and "the benevolent influence of the Great Russian people and its culture."[34] By the same token, one may as well argue that Britain unified India, that she was more civilized than India's Asian neighbors and that she enabled India to establish a state of its own, the British Indian Empire. The similarity of Soviet defense of Russian colonization to that of British and French is striking.

After Stalin's death, however, the cultural pressure on Soviet Moslems was somewhat reduced. Bagirov, prime minister of Azerbaijan, who initiated the implementation of Zhdanov's ideas by starting the 1950 anti-Shamil campaign, was demoted and later liquidated as Beria's agent.[35] The question was reopened and the 1956 discussion showed a division among Soviet historians.[36] It is now again possible to say that the Russian conquest was not always enthusiastically accepted. However, the basic tenets of the theory of "absolute good" of the Russian conquest of the Caucasus and of Central Asia have not been revised, and no return to Pokrovsky's theory of "absolute evil" of colonial conquest seems in sight, although in 1961 Pokrovsky was again favorably mentioned in the Soviet press.

Education

During the years of the Soviet regime, political considerations notwithstanding, achievements in the field of education in Central Asia have been impressive. Equal educational opportunities have been provided to Russian and Moslem children. The development of the school system and of literacy has been remarkable,[37] although not as high as the Soviet figures indicate. In 1910 there were only 100,000 native pupils in native schools in Russian Turkestan. In addition, 130,000 pupils attended scholastically backward religious schools in the emirate of Bukhara and 22,500 in the khanate of Khiva.[38] Together they amounted to less than one-fifth of the students in Uzbekistan alone in the 1940's.

By 1941 official school attendance in Uzbekistan was five times higher than that in Iran in 1952 and close to the 1950 figures of some southern states in the United States.[39]

The high percentage of literacy in Central Asia is due to the strongly developed compulsory school system and to the mass campaigns launched against adult illiteracy. The percentage of literacy in Central Asia is much higher than elsewhere in the Moslem Middle and Near East.[40] Many experts, however, consider Soviet literacy claims as highly exaggerated. Dubicki, a Polish émigré who lived in that area, estimates the proportion of literate natives in the 1940's at 30 per cent and the adult literacy at only 7 or 10 per cent.[41] The English expert, Lieutenant Colonel G. E. Wheeler, considers the percentage of literacy to be around 50 per cent (in the early 1950's).[42] Gayet, a French authority, considers official Soviet figures "unbelievable" and "improbable." The explanation lies presumably in the fact that the official literacy statistics seem to include semiliterate people who are barely able to sign their names or spell more than a few words. This group may possibly account for one-half of the total "literate" people.[43] Also unknown, in contrast to the 1926 census, is the proportion of Russians and other Europeans among literate people in Central Asia according to the 1939 and 1959 censuses.

Elementary-school attendance in Central Asia in the 1940's was more or less the same among European and native boys. However, thousands of Moslem school-age children in rural areas did not attend schools;[44] and among secondary-school, college and university students, natives were strongly under-represented. This situation cannot be attributed to a lack of encouragement, but rather to the still existing gap in cultural levels between Russian and native communities. As a result, Uzbek students amounted to only 32.5 per cent of the total enrollment at the University of Central Asia in Tashkent (SAGU) in 1940, and Kazakh students only 30 per cent of the total at the University of Alma-Ata. Among 2,200 students who graduated from high schools in Uzbekistan in 1943, only 500 were of Uzbek nationality.[45] However, by 1961 natives of Central Asia and Kazakhstan accounted for over one-third of the students in universities, institutes and technical schools in the area. Taking into consideration that no universities existed in Central Asia before the Revolution, the presence of 250,000 students in the institutions of higher learning in Central Asia in 1961, even if two-thirds of them were of European origin, is a remarkable achievement.[46]

Soviet educational statistics are especially impressive in regard to Moslem women, who, before the Revolution, took no part in public life. According to official figures, they are more active in public life than women in any other Moslem country in the Middle East. General Tubert, a French Communist sympathizer who visited Uzbekistan in 1950, reported that 15,000 Uzbek women worked as teachers, 3,000 as engineers, technicians and managers, 233 as doctors or university graduates, and 213 as chairmen of collective farms.[47] Under closer analysis these figures appear misleading. At that time there were 10,000 Uzbek specialists and technicians in the republic, 0.4 per cent of them women. Therefore the total number of native women specialists was only 40, and the figures given by Tubert must be inaccurate. The number of women chairmen of collective farms also looks less impressive if one knows that they constitute only 2.5 per cent of the total number of collective-farm chairmen in the republic.[48] The attendance of Moslem girls in secondary schools and universities is acknowledged to be poor.[49] According to Bennigsen, Moslem girls constituted only 2 or 3 per cent of the students in secondary schools and universities in Central Asia in the 1950's, while in Egypt women make up 12 per cent of the student body in similar institutions.[50] Although, undoubtedly, the situation of women in Central Asia has greatly improved since the Revolution, a similar change occurred in other Moslem lands with neither Communism nor alien guidance and supervision.

Turkestani nationalists see a direct correlation between Soviet socio-economic achievements and the policy of Russification. "Sovietization, industrialization, Russification" was the sequence of events, they say.[51]

However, the transformation brought by Soviet Russia in her Central Asian possessions cannot, and should not, be judged as negative by the sole yardstick of "Russification." As stated by Richard Pipes, a Harvard specialist on Central Asian affairs:

. . . The social and cultural processes occurring in Soviet Central Asia do not differ fundamentally from those taking place in other colonial or ex-colonial areas of the world. In both instances native societies, under the impact of European culture, become secularized, westernized.[52]

Western observers traveling in Central Asia were impressed by the conformity of the life in that area to everything European Russian, as well as by the presence of Russian officials side by side with native office holders:

Moscow's grip—when I say "Moscow's grip," I mean the Western grip and imprint on these regions—is both obvious and depressing. The Party organizations, the format and the contents of newspapers, the programmes in the opera houses . . . the theatre play-bills, the same old slogans in the Parks of Culture and Rest; the restaurants with their frightfully slow service, where even food has little of local variety except mediocre shashlik and pilaff; the stores, a fly-blown replica of the poorer stores in Moscow; the same kind of bookshops and the same books; the large number of Western Russian officials (*every official of Central Asian nationality seems to have a Western Russian opposite number*); the presence of Western Russian troops and frontier guards—in every way there is undeniable evidence of the control of that area by Western Russia.

There is certainly no colour-bar. On the other hand, encouragement of local minority cultures, about which we hear so much in Soviet propaganda, is an extremely limited matter, mostly confined to rather precious art displays, folk dancing, production of odd newspapers in the local language and so on.[53]

Yet individual Russians were never granted the superior status which characterized the old European standing in Asian or African society. This remained the single most important positive factor in Russian-Moslem relations, despite the flaws in the much propagandized Soviet "friendship of peoples" and even despite the reality of the Soviet Russian presence in Central Asia.

Chapter 7

The Cadres, the Elite, and the People

The Purges of the 1930's

IN 1921 STALIN GAVE an interesting definition of the Soviet system of government. He began by comparing it with the only administration he had known before, the tsarist autocracy:

There are two ways of governing a country. One way is to have a simplified apparatus headed by a group of people, or by a single person, having hands and eyes in localities in the shape of governors. This is a very simple form of government, under which the ruler, in governing the country, receives the kind of information governors can supply, and consoles himself with the hope that he is governing honestly and well. Frictions arise, frictions pass into conflicts and conflicts into revolts. The revolts are then crushed. This is not our system of government, it is too costly.

Stalin then explained what he considered to be the best means of ruling the state:

In our Soviet country we must evolve a system of government which will permit us with certainty to anticipate all changes, to perceive everything that is going on among peasants, the non-Russian nationals and the Russians; the system of barometers which will anticipate every change, register and forestall a Basmachi movement, Kronstadt, and all possible storms and ill-fortune.[1]

The system envisaged by Stalin developed itself along four principal channels of command and control: the Party organization, the government bureaucracy, the armed forces and the police apparatus. The Party was designed to be the promoter, the vanguard and the driving force of the system; the bureaucracy, its executive arm; the army, its sword against the outside menace; the police apparatus, its sword against the internal enemies of the regime.

The main driving force of this system, the Communist Party, during the years of Stalin's rule, was practically deprived of its leading position and reduced to the function of another executive arm of the system, parallel to that of the governmental bureaucracy. The "cult of personality" (that is, the complete subservience to the person in command) dominant in the Party exercised a paralyzing effect on the Party membership as well as on the Party apparatus, and resulted in the bureaucratization and stratification of the entire structure. Party officials were afraid of responsibility, of possible errors, and consequently lacked initiative. The purge became the only way for renovating the Party cadres and for injecting fresh forces into its otherwise stratified body. The medicine was, however, defective in itself: the fear of the purge reduced Party officials to the very state of immobility against which the purge had initially been brought into action. The best Party men often fell victim to such indiscriminate purges, while those who should have been removed managed to survive. This state of affairs worked against the ideal theoretical concept of the Party as the general staff of the socialist revolution, the leading and directing force of Soviet society, the Party of the proletariat and the association of the "best people" in Soviet society.[2]

In accordance with the theoretical principles, the Communist Party was presumed to select its members from among the most "revolutionarily conscious" workers, ideally those with proven leadership abilities. This may well have been the case in the early days of the Revolution. It was not the case in Central Asia, where the Communist parties of all the five republics were in a shaky condition, most of their vitality having been sapped by the purges of the 1930's.

From 1930 to 1938 seven successive purges destroyed almost all the fragile local Communist Party cadres. Noteworthy among the liquidated were N. Maksum (1933) and Shotemar (1937), presidents of Tajikistan; Khodzhaev and Rakhimbabaev (1937), premiers of Tajikistan; U. Kulambetov (1935) and U. Isayev (1938), premiers of Kazakhstan; Y. Abdurakhmanov, premier of Kirgizia; Faizulla Khodzhaev, former head of the government of the People's Republic of Bukhara (1922–24) and chairman of the Council of People's Commissars of Uzbekistan (1924–37); Akmal Ikramov (1937), first secretary of the Communist Party of Uzbekistan; T. Ryskulov, vicepremier of the Russian republic, former premier of Soviet Turkestan; a number of political figures of lesser stature and scores of officials and intellectuals. In the purge of 1937, 55.7 per cent of the Party officials in primary Party organizations and 70.8 per cent in district Party committees were replaced by new people.[3] Among the purged, Faizulla Khodzhaev was the outstanding personality. He "confessed" that he had joined the Right Opposition (Bukharin and his friends) because the latter would guarantee the independence of the Uzbek Republic. He was then forced to declare:

. . . even if it would become possible at the price of black treachery, at the price of treason to the fatherland . . . it goes without saying that this fictitious independence would have been a new disaster to the peoples of Uzbekistan.[4]

At the government level, after the removal of Khodzhaev (July, 1937) three successive Uzbek premiers were ousted in less than a year. Abdulla Karimov lasted two weeks, Torabekov a few weeks and Soltan Segisbaev half a year.[5] All were liquidated as enemies of the people, while at the same time thousands of their followers were purged. The potential or imaginary danger of national Communism was thus eliminated, but the cost for the Party was a heavy one: native Party cadres, after the storm of 1937–38, became weaker and less efficient than ever and, consequently, more dependent upon outside (Russian) guardianship. The process of rebuilding the native cadres, in progress in 1939–40, had not yet achieved completion when the Soviet Union found herself at war with Germany.

The Party Elite in the 1940's

The most powerful element among the Communist Party membership has always been the so-called Party elite (*aktiv*). The difference between the elite and grass-roots Party membership is of great significance. The first, often called the Party-Soviet collective farm elite or Party-economic elite, consists of members of the Party hierarchy and actually is the Soviet "ruling class." Its members have the support of the Party organization in dealing with the workers, and "the director relies on the Party organization and the Party organization supports the director in all his measures."[6]

The wartime situation in the Uzbek city of Samarkand serves as a good example of the state of affairs existing all over Central Asia. In Samarkand the Party elite roughly amounted to one-fourth of the total Party membership (800 out of 2,900).[7] The remaining three-fourths of the members, persons of lower Party standing, provided a link between the elite and the mass of nonmembers. An analysis of the national composition of the Samarkand managerial elite shows that chairmen of the collective farms in the region (*oblast*) had been exclusively native (no Russian collective farms existed in the region at that time). In all other managerial positions Russians, Ukrainians and other Europeans were in the majority. In industry, in five out of seven large factories in Samarkand City during the early 1940's the directors were Europeans, and in one out of seven they were Europeans during half the period. Of the remaining twenty-three Samarkand factories, seven had European directors all the time, five had European directors part of the time, and only six were in native Moslem hands during the whole war period. In five of eight trusts on which data were found and analyzed, the directors were Europeans, in two they were Europeans half of the time, and only in one was the director a native for the entire period. (No data were available for five factories.) In the cooperatives of regional importance, the ratio was four Europeans to three natives.[8] At the same time the Tashkent newspaper *Pravda Vostoka* disclosed the poor educational level of factory directors in Samarkand: in 1941, out of thirty-one directors, twenty-three never went beyond the first four grades of elementary school and only three were engineers. Only three directors were Uzbeks at that time.[9] These managers were, for the most part, Party members. Thus the national composition of the managerial class was identical with that of the Party elite.

Similarly, as on the regional level, native officials on the district level (*raion*) were replaced, whenever necessary, by more efficient, more skilled and more reliable Russians or other European officials. This happened in the district of Zaamin, where a Russian was substituted for the native first secretary for the duration of the war. This was also the case in many factories in the city of Samarkand.

The same happened in several other Party and economic organizations, in various districts, and on different levels. It should be added that the local press carefully avoided criticizing native Moslem inefficiency, although such criticism was often voiced by Russian officials in private conversations. Newspaper articles dealing with the shortcomings of Uzbek officials invariably mentioned the short-comings of Russian, Ukrainian, or other European officials, even if the failure of the latter was on a much smaller scale.

The party elite of each community was given the re-sponsibility of insuring political conformity of its own people. In addition, the Russian Party elite had the task of helping its less experienced native counterpart and of keeping an eye on native nationalist elements, whether of Basmachi or of national-Communist origin. The natives, aware of the situation, felt no hostility toward the native Communists. On the contrary, they regarded them as protectors and allies against the Russian chauvinists and against the hardships imposed by the regime. Native Mos-lem confidence in Moslem Communists was, however, an advantage to the Soviet regime itself. For the Communist Party was then able to use the native Communists more effectively. It would have been very difficult indeed to administer the area properly had the native Communists been regarded by their own people as Russian puppets, thereby making the reality of Soviet colonial rule visible to everyone. Thus Soviet authorities, if they were to avoid serious trouble, were obliged to overlook some of the less objectionable nationalist practices.

The Communist leaders were willing to employ force to make the Uzbeks plant cotton, but not to make them treat their women according to the Western standards.[10]

The oriental regard for personal prestige and "face" was taken into consideration by the Party. "The Party is being tactful; Russians occupy the key jobs, but local people who can be trusted are given prominence and responsibility," explains an English visitor.[11]

Similarly, the Soviet regime tolerated minor abuses of power by native Party officials and managers, as long as they were directed against a particular Russian, because it provided a scapegoat for otherwise frustrated nationalist sentiments. Thus some Moslem collective-farm chairmen delighted in bullying European refugees (Poles included) in the 1940's. Certain Moslem factory directors abused their authority in dealing with Europeans.

Russian experience with Asiatic peoples has been rich and intimate, and the Russians are unusually free from attitudes of "racial" snobbery, although some condescension toward technically less advanced peoples has developed in recent decades,[12]

explains an American expert, commenting on Russian racial tolerance toward persons of Asian origin. One can possibly argue that the policy of Russification conducted by the Soviet Union in Central Asia cannot be considered an aim in itself, but rather a result of a clash between "a highly centralized regime," which happens to be Russian, and the "nationalities" molded by its absolute power.

Experts assume that between 1936 and 1941 a policy of recruiting Party candidates from among the upper groups of Soviet society prevailed.[13] During these years the workers were gradually forced into a position of inferior status within the Party ranks. Then, with the beginning of World War II, this policy was supposedly abandoned and the new policy of "mass wartime recruitment had the net result of giving the Party firmer roots in the lower reaches of the Soviet society."[14] Such recruitment was generally conducted in the army units, but a large number of native Central Asian draftees, because of their known lack of enthusiasm, were sent to labor units, where no mass Party recruitment took place.[15]

In Uzbekistan the proportion of factory workers within the Party remained small. Even in highly industrialized

Tashkent, only one-fourth of the new Party candidates admitted in 1946 were workers.[16] It is true that a policy of mass recruitment was conducted among the soldiers on the front and that the 1945–46 demobilization brought home thousands of Communist recruits.[17] But from January 1, 1945, to July 1, 1946, the percentage of workers among the newly recruited Party members had risen to only 26.6.[18] The more able elements among the Party working-class recruits were soon incorporated into the managerial elite, thus eliminating the danger of a competing proletarian elite arising from within the Party. In 1946 the Communist Party of Uzbekistan remained a managerial Party with weak working-class connections. This situation still prevailed in the late 1950's and even after the Twentieth Party Congress of 1956.[19]

The Party in the villages had even weaker popular roots than in the city. Many collective farms had no Party primary organizations.[20] In many smaller farms the chairman was the only Party member. In larger collective farms, where the number of Party members was higher, the Party membership remained limited to the managerial personnel, and Party cards were seldom held by average farmers. The Tashkent Regional Party Committee discloses that during 1945, 19 collective-farm chairmen, 12 farm managers and 111 heads of brigades were admitted to the Party in the rural areas of the Tashkent region. The number of rank-and-file farmers admitted was not mentioned, since the Party in the villages was representative of the new rural socio-economic elite (those people deriving their higher status from the collective-farm policy imposed by the Communist regime).[21]

In one particularly large collective farm the Party organization numbered eleven persons (seven members and four candidates) who were all Moslems and members of the rural elite—the chairman, the deputy chairman, three managers, the secretary of the primary Party organization, the director of the Agitation and Propaganda Center, two local school teachers and two brigade heads.[22]

In another collective farm with 325 households there were five Party members and eight candidates: the chairman, the secretary of the primary Party organization and three brigade heads.[23] An identical situation prevailed in the collective farms of the Zaamin district.

Nor was the situation in state farms and MTS Machine-Tractor Stations) any different. Party membership was limited to the managing personnel, while the rank-and-file employees remained outside the Party. In fact, in the entire Uzbek Republic in 1946 only 1 per cent of Party members in rural areas were tractor drivers. Only sixteen combine operators throughout all of Uzbekistan were Party members (that is, about two per region).[24] New recruitment was very slow. It was disclosed that only eight tractor drivers and no combine operators were accepted into the Party in the Tashkent region during the year 1945.[25] Unlike the farm chairmen, the MTS directors in the Samarkand region were mostly Russians or other Europeans. Among the thirty-five MTS of the region, sixteen had European directors and ten had European directors half of the time, while only nine had native directors throughout the entire war period. In the particular case of the Zaamin district with three MTS, the first had a European director during the whole period, the second from 1944 on, and the third from the end of the war on.[26] An MTS with a native director generally had a European in charge of its political department (and vice versa). The Europeans were also predominant among the state-farm management. In the district of Zaamin the directors of the two large state grain farms (one of them Udarnik, the largest in Uzbekistan) were Europeans.[27] A number of European settlers were employed in state farms and MTS mainly because of a shortage of skilled workers (especially tractor drivers and combine operators) among the Moslems.

Several chains of control were established in the village in order to insure proper functioning of the collective-farm system. In the Party chain, the work of the collective-farm board and of its chairman was supervised by the collective-farm Party organization, and the latter was supervised by the Party organization of the local MTS, responsible for several farms in the neighborhood. The district departments of agriculture controlled the collective farms both directly and through the reports of the local MTS, in whose hands was concentrated the indispensable farm machinery.[28] The executive committee of the District Soviet exercised its control through the chain of village Soviets. In turn the district Party committee supervised the work of all the above-listed organizations and allocated grain delivery quotas among the collective farms. In addition, it kept itself busy interfering directly in most other matters.

On top of all these local controls, the collective farm could expect further trouble from inspectors representing one or another of the bureaucratic agencies at the regional level. The latter were eager to check the situation on the spot, bypassing the district officials who were often guilty of exaggerating production achievements and hiding shortcomings. A number of articles in the Tashkent newspaper *Pravda Vostoka* dealt with this subject: "The Humbugs from Khatyrchi" (September 12, 1943), "Squandering of Cattle Under the Name of 'Other Expenses'" (July 19, 1944), "Swindlers Patronized in Ak-Darya" (June 24, 1944).

Quite often the guilty were brought before the courts,[29] but graft, thievery and waste were much too widespread to permit a clean sweep to take place. It was difficult to break the profitable "family circles" of local officials in the rural areas. *Pravda Vostoka* relates a story of a rural Inspector K. who found pilfering and graft in the local consumers' cooperative, village Soviet and collective farms. Although K. presented conclusive evidence to the district attorney and to the Party officials, no serious action was ever taken against the guilty ones. The reason was obvious: K. had taken the wrong step of attacking the brother and the close friends of the local district Party secretary.[30] This state of affairs became common in the early 1940's because of wartime shortages and inflation. Firing of responsible managers was not a good remedy. During one year, out of thirty-five directors of MTS in the Samarkand region, thirteen were replaced. In some districts, such changes occurred two or three times a year.[31] During the first three months of 1944, the Regional Department of Agriculture in Samarkand replaced twelve agronomists, eleven mechanics, four district managers, four MTS directors and five MTS bookkeepers, but failed to put a stop to the illegal spare-parts traffic going on within the local MTS system. At the same time almost all of the MTS fell short of the plan during the spring sowing campaign.[32] The turnover of collective-farm chairmen was similarly high. In one of the districts of the Fergana region, reported the newspaper, twenty-eight chairmen had been replaced in a four-month period. In most of the cases their removal was due to incompetence.[33] In one case the man fired had been forced upon the farmers only two months before. Strange as it may seem, a chairman who failed in his job was often transferred—to the chairmanship of another farm.[34] However, a case of extreme failure usually ended in court.[35]

The Party had to content itself with the available human material. Better-qualified men were scarce in the local officialdom, and economic conditions, especially in wartime, were such that even able people deteriorated fast under the impact of pressures, demands, threats, shortages, inefficiency and inflation.

The Native Moslem Party Member

No image of the Party organization in Central Asia would be complete without a description of the individual native Party member, his background, his social status within his own community, his relations with Russians, his motives in joining the Party and the degree of his devotion to the Communist cause.

Stalin, in order to make the Central Asian Republics "national in form, but socialist in content," proclaimed a line to be followed by the Soviet regime in that area:

1. To create industrial centers . . . as bases on which peasants can be rallied around the working-class. . . .

2. To advance agriculture and above all irrigation.

3. To improve and advance co-operative organization among the broad masses of the peasants and handicraftsmen as the most reliable way of bringing the Soviet Republics of the East into the general system of Soviet economic development.

4. To bring the Soviets into close touch with the masses; to make them national in composition, and in this way to implant a national Soviet state organization that will be close and comprehensive to the toiling masses.

5. To develop national culture; to build up a wide system of courses and schools for both general education, and vocational and technical training in native languages, with the purpose of training Soviet party, trade union, and economic cadres among the native people.[36]

In order to achieve these goals, an understanding of nationalist aspirations was, according to Stalin, essential:

Russian Communists cannot combat Tatar, Georgian, or Bashkir chauvinism [read: "nationalism"], for if the Russian Communists were to undertake this difficult task . . . it would be regarded as a fight of a Great Russian chauvinism against the Tatars or the Georgians. This would confuse the whole issue. . . . Only Georgian Communists can successfully combat Georgian nationalism.[37]

Native Communists were bound, moreover, to remember that ideological and political conformity with Moscow's orders had to be observed. As was pointed out in *Pravda* one year after the end of World War II: "The whole Uzbek people, young and old, will remember for all time that it owes its achievements to the Party of Lenin and Stalin, to its elder brother the Russian people."[38] This idea was expressed as early as 1929, when one of the Soviet leaders, Mikhail Kalinin, trying to put the objectives of the Soviet policy in Central Asia into simple words, said that its aim was "teaching the people of the Kirgiz Steppe, the small Uzbek cotton grower, and the Turkmenian gardener the ideals of the Leningrad worker."[39]

Between that time and the beginning of World War II a social revolution along Stalin's lines developed in Central Asia with the collectivization of agriculture, three five-year plans, a large Russian immigration, small purges, the "Great Purge," antireligious campaigns, campaigns against "local nationalism," campaigns for the "liberation of women," campaigns for eradication of illiteracy, reforms of alphabets, reforms of local administration, constitutional changes, and a number of other changes, campaigns, reforms, and plans, too numerous and too varied to be listed.

The "small Uzbek cotton grower" was forced to join a collective farm, his son went to work in the city, his daughter took off the veil, his *mullah* was sent away, and one or two among his more opportunistic relatives joined the ruling party. Many times he had to thank his "big brother" and teacher "for making his people cultured and happy."[40] He avoided open opposition to big brother's ideals, but received the news about the German attack upon Russia with a slight hope that something good might come out of big brother's trouble, only to find himself working harder than ever for Russia's victory.

Most of the native Moslems belonging to the Party during the 1940's were members of the socio-economic elite. They were chairmen of collective farms, brigadiers, factory directors, office managers, local Party officials, administrators and people of similar status. These people had living standards far higher than the average and enjoyed priorities and advantages commensurate with their position. They had, one can say, a vested interest in the smooth functioning of the Soviet regime, both in the fulfillment of its production plans and in the success of its propaganda campaigns. They owed the positions they occupied to the regime in power.

Here the question may be asked whether the native Party members were recruited from the socio-economic elite or promoted into it only after having joined the Party. Actually, the Party picked its recruits from among those natives who showed a readiness to obey and to execute Party orders, who possessed an ability to command, an eagerness to learn from the Russians the more advanced "Western" methods of organization, a better than average intelligence and a lack of scruples, all connected with a strong inner drive to succeed. Although better-educated people were eagerly sought, lack of education was not an obstacle to a Party career.[41] Those selected were, following their admission into the Party, speedily promoted to positions of responsibility.

The following case, taken from a local newspaper editorial, illustrates the way such speedy promotions were handled:

A short time ago K . . . was a rank and file member of the collective farm . . . After having entered the Party, under the guidance of the Party organization, K . . . started to work more actively, showed more initiative, became more demanding of herself. This led to her promotion to the leading job, that of vice-chairman of the collective farm.[42]

This example suggests that a direct correlation exists between the promotion to an executive position and the possession of a Party card.

New members recruited from among those in managerial positions were first in line for promotion. The new Party member had no choice but to show his zeal for his job and for the Party, which gave him his promotion. Bad will or obvious failures could lead to serious troubles, including demotion or even ejection from the Party. A person expelled from the Party was in a worse position than one who had never applied for admission. But the Party could not be too demanding either, since the number of natives who possessed the minimum qualifications for Party membership was so small. Many of the better-qualified natives had either been involved in the Basmachi revolt or had fled abroad. Others, already members of the Party, had fallen victim to the purges of the late 1930's.

Consequently, the native Party members of the 1940's were mainly persons who had joined the Party after the purge of the old members. They knew little about Communism and cared even less. They hardly knew who Marx and Lenin were. In any case, they valued leadership for its own sake and enjoyed the pleasure of command in a truly oriental way.[43]

Even in the late 1950's many native Party leaders, with the exception of those on the highest level, maintained Moslem social habits so often condemned by the regime.[44] These included secluding women,[45] prearranging marriages and maintaining the custom of *kalym* (payment for the bride). As described by a foreign expert in the mid-1950's:

Cases of polygamy among Komsomols, directors of *kolkhozes*, and local officials of the Party have been cited. Moslem Communists continue to keep their wives in harems, even if the latter become presidents of the Soviet or directors of cooperatives.[46]

The aversion to pork, the observing of the most important of Moslem religious holidays and the slow oriental way of life remained widespread. "We have been happy in Samarkand for many, many years. Allah is good, the soil is rich, and one is blessed with many children. Why have discontent and all these meetings and reading and writing? It is not necessary,"[47] says a well-to-do Uzbek to an English traveler. An equally traditional point of view is expressed by a village elder who, answering a question about women picking cotton in the field, concluded:

"These need no spare parts, no maintenance and work well. Why have machines?"[48]

"Russians and Moslems live side by side but do not mix," remarks Bennigsen, who goes on arguing that Moslem intellectuals, even when "de-Islamized," cannot be assimilated by the Russians to adopt their way of life, but remain attached to their own ways,[49] at least as far as their private lives are concerned.

During the war years the nationalist state of mind led to a recrudescence of local chauvinism. The reminiscence of the behavior of the Soviet Russian troops during the civil war was not helping the Soviet cause. The "Kokand pogrom," the "Bukhara robbery," and the "Katta-Kurgan vodka bath" were not easy to forget. Purges of "bourgeois nationalists" in the 1930's and the emphasis placed upon Great Russian patriotism in the 1940's did not help to erase old impressions from the minds of the natives. Clearly those memories accounted, to a large extent, for their lack of enthusiasm to die for Russia during World War II.[50] Thousands of Central Asian draftees deserted the Red Army or enrolled in pro-German Turkestan units when taken as prisoners of war.[51] Draft dodgers, numerous among the natives, were not viewed unsympathetically by their own people. Russian military commissars in charge of local draft boards seemed fully aware of the situation. Frequent raffles were organized in markets and other public places in order to catch deserters. After Stalingrad it became a prevailing practice to direct Moslem draftees to the so-called "labor front" (work brigades) instead of sending them to the fighting forces. Local newspapers were, however, full of accounts about the heroic deeds of native soldiers fighting the Germans in the front line. Although a number of Central Asian natives fought at the front and fought well, there is little doubt that only a minority of Moslem draftees was entrusted with combat duty.

This situation is described by a Turkestani émigré, Baymirza Hayit,[52] but unfortunately, his accounts contain a number of unfounded allegations. While Hayit rightly stresses the fact that many Moslems deserted into the mountains of Central Asia to escape the draft, his descriptions of the same deserters conducting guerrilla warfare against the Russians are not confirmed by other writers or by the Polish refugees, then scattered throughout the area. The June 23, 1943, attack on the Tashkent garrison by some ten thousand Moslem inhabitants of that city, as described by Hayit, is unknown and unheard of, even by people who lived in Tashkent at that time. Native wartime lack of enthusiasm for the Russian cause took a much more cautious and less heroic path.

Just as everywhere else in the world, personal connections are of great importance in the Soviet Union. Known in Russia by the colloquial name of *blat,* they are the sesame which opens the door and untangles the red tape. In Soviet Central Asia, following this pattern, mutual assistance between Moslem managers and administrators in cases involving personal conflicts with Russians (officials as well as others) was widespread during the 1940's. There was mutual on-the-job favoritism resembling a similar tendency among the Russians. In some remote regions, close-knit friends ran the collective farms in their traditional way, while government inspectors were often successfully bribed away. In the cultural field influential natives tried to impose the use of their own language along with Russian in offices, factories and administration. Many "Westernized" Moslems showed a conspicuous attachment to local traditions in dress, food and manners, visibly stressing their solidarity with the native masses. The tendency to seek refuge in their own cultural heritage, pre-Russian history, Moslem legends, popular songs and native art was widespread among the intellectuals.

The regime was well aware of the unpleasant implications of such practices and did its utmost to eradicate them. Its best insurance against "mutual assistance" among native executives was the system of reserving selected key positions in the Party, government and economy for Russians, and of providing every important native official with a Russian aide. The use of the Russian language in all office work (collective farms excepted) forced even native chauvinists to learn Russian. The practical autonomy of the remote collective farms was undermined by the tightening of state control. Attempting to achieve social integration of the native society, the regime extolled the "Western" way of life and branded the traditional Moslem way as backward and reactionary.

Despite Party efforts, the two principal communities in Central Asia, the Moslem and the Russian, never became integrated. Each lives its own life and seldom mixes with the other.

Chapter 8

The Party Apparatus (Uzbekistan As an Example)

The Secretariat of the Central Committee
The 1940's

THE HIGHEST AUTHORITY in every Union Republic of the USSR is the central committee of its Communist party, but more especially its secretariat. It is the real seat of power and, at the same time, the watchdog of the Central Committee of the Communist Party of the Soviet Union in the given republic. This is in full conformity with the Moscow pattern, where the Central Committee, during the days of Stalin, was completely overshadowed by its *Politbureau* (now Presidium) and its secretariat. As the head of the latter, Stalin gained the upper hand in the Party and the government. The secretariat possesses an elaborate structure with special emphasis given to the departments supervising industry and farming.

During the war years the political part of the secretariat of the Central Committee of the Uzbek Republic was composed of five secretaries—the first, second and third secretaries, the secretary for propaganda and agitation, and the secretary for cadres' administration—and three department heads: the chief of the Organization-Instruction Department (now Department of Party Organs), the chief of the Military Department and the chief of the Special Section. Although a section is a subdivision of a department, the Special (Police) Section, by virtue of its importance, is generally considered separately.

The numerous economic departments of the secretariat

may be more conveniently divided into three groups: heavy industries and power, consumer goods, and agriculture.

The first group included six major departments whose major task was the supervision of those branches of economy essential to the war effort; the second group included departments dealing mainly with branches of economy engaged in the production of goods and commodities for local use and consumption; the third group consisted of departments taking care of the main branches of farming (see Table 6).

Among the eight "political" positions in the secretariat, five were held by Russians and other Europeans throughout the war period. These included the second and third secretaries and the powerful chiefs of the Organization-Instruction Department, the Military Department and the Special Section. Moslems were assigned to three positions only: those of the first secretary and the secretaries for cadres' administration, for propaganda and for agitation, all of which involved direct contact with the native population.

Of the twelve economic departments, only two were put in Moslem hands.[1] The usual pattern of having a deputy of different nationality from that of the department chief was generally observed. Of the twenty-two major positions in the Uzbek Central Committee's secretariat, only six were held by natives, an almost four-to-one ratio in favor of the Europeans. These figures show that the native Communists were left in a minority within the leading body of their "own" Party organization.

The 1950's

As to the continuity of the wartime situation, a comparison with the contemporary state of affairs is revealing. The wartime situation might, after all, have been dictated by the emergencies of the moment. The death of Stalin, the Twentieth Party Congress, and the resulting liberalization of policy toward minorities might conceivably have changed the situation. There is little evidence to support this contention, however.

There has been almost no relaxation of Soviet Russian control over and within the local Party apparatus in Uzbekistan; the key Party positions are still held by Russians and other Europeans. In the Central Committee's secretariat the position of second secretary has never been out of Russian hands.[2] As stated by Bennigsen in 1959:

The first secretary, who is the prominent figure, *is always* and *everywhere* a "national," while the second secretary, who is also *secretary of the cadres* and thus in control of the entire Party hierarchy, and therefore the real head of the entire Party hierarchy, *is always* and everywhere a Russian.[3]

The combination of the positions of second secretary and secretary for cadres' administration seems to be a new development, strengthening the Russian control over the Central Committee. During the war years the position of the secretary for cadres' administration was a separate one, usually held by a native. The recent change visibly enhanced the already powerful position of the Russian second secretary.

The proportion of Europeans among the members of the Central Committee itself (31 per cent in Uzbekistan, 58.4 in Kazakhstan, 34 in Kirgizstan, 38.5 in Turkmenistan and 25.3 in Tajikistan, all for 1958) indicates the strength of Russian officialdom if the allocation of positions along national lines is taken into consideration.[4] The percentage of Europeans in the secretariats of the respective central committees is higher and runs from 50 per cent in Kirgizstan to 40–44.3 per cent in all other Central Asian Republics.[5]

This situation attracted the attention of the British observer of Central Asian affairs, Walter Z. Laqueur:

> Soviet domestic policy . . . is still dominated by a profound distrust towards the indigenous elements in the Central Asiatic Republics. The key positions in these areas have remained in the hands of Party secretaries of Russian origin. . . . Moreover . . . these Russian functionaries have remained at their posts while wholesale purges have taken place among the native leadership.[6]

Under such conditions one can hardly compare the Communist parties of Eastern Europe with those of Soviet Central Asia. In the former case, we deal with "national-Communist" parties with a variable degree of dependence on Moscow. In the second case there is no national party in the strict sense of the word. Since the Party has been established on a territorial and not on a national basis, its Moslem members are not only faced with Russian control from Moscow, but from their own capital as well, where Russians and other outsiders are in firm control of the Party apparatus.

The Government and the Party

The Party supremacy over parallel governmental organs is a basic tenet of the Soviet system. According to Soviet experts on public administration, this supremacy is founded on the following principles:

1. The leading Party and government hierarchy have been fused.
2. The Party has control over elections and appointments.
3. Not a single important problem is solved without appropriate Party instructions. Matters of great importance are dealt with by joint resolutions of the Party's Central Committee and of the Council of Ministers.

4. The Party determines and directs the drafting of plans.
5. Party groups exist in all Soviet organs. They are responsible for keeping the Party line among non-Party people.
6. Party members, regardless of their position, are subject to Party control and discipline.
7. Party organs supervise the work of corresponding state administrations and, through local Party organizations, enforce Party decisions down to enterprise, office and collective-farm level.[7]

This superior position has been maintained by the Party through all the levels of the administrative ladder—from the Kremlin to the district administration in the remotest region of Central Asia. According to the above-listed official definitions, the Party is definitely "more equal" (to use George Orwell's expression) than the government. The latter remains, however, the main executive body, while the Party directs and controls its activity. The work of the Council of Ministers of a Union Republic consists mainly in carrying out directives received from the central government in Moscow. As stated by a Western expert, Julian Towster, "The extraordinary scope of federal powers makes it difficult to see where any policy-making prerogative is left within the Union Republic."[8]

This is especially true since the Union Republic's budget, including all its important details, is prepared in Moscow.

The 1940's

The "Stalin Constitution," as of the beginning of World War II, distinguished two kinds of ministries in the Union Republics:

1. Autonomous ministries (that is, without a central

Moscow counterpart) conducting purely local operations and dependent on Moscow only in matters of basic laws and policy principles set out by the central government. Such were the Ministries (known prior to 1946 as "people's commissariats") of Social Security, Local Industry and Communal Economy, and later, also those of Education and Highway Transportation.

2. Subordinated ministries (subordinated to the corresponding central ministries in Moscow) conducting local operations under Moscow's planning and supervision. This group included all the remaining ministries.

On the local levels the employees of both autonomous and subordinated ministries were paid by regional, district or city authorities. The Ministries of Justice, State Security and Internal Affairs, because of security aspects involved in their operations, took care of selecting and paying their own personnel. A number of important matters, such as supplies, foreign affairs, foreign trade, transportation and communication, water transportation, defense, heavy industry and machine industry, were handled directly from Moscow since no corresponding ministries existed at the Union Republic level. The officials of these central ministries, operating at local levels, were directly responsible to the central authorities, bypassing all local administration.[9] During the war a number of special representatives of central ministries operated in Central Asia, channeling the demands of their local agents directly to Moscow and pressuring local authorities for manpower, raw materials and all sorts of priorities.

Ministerial positions in the wartime Council of Ministers may be also conveniently divided into three groups: general administration, industry and trade, and agriculture. The general administration group (eleven positions) included the prime minister (at that time chairman of the Council of People's Commissars), assisted by three or more deputies, and the people's commissars (later ministers) in charge of justice, internal affairs, state security, state control, finance, social security, public health, education, foreign affairs (since 1944) and the head of the Union Republic's State Planning Commission. Eleven ministries were concerned with industry and commerce and four ministries were in charge of farming, cattle breeding[10] and irrigation (see Table 6).

In Uzbekistan the office of the chairman of the Council of Ministers has always been held by an Uzbek. Together with the chairmanship of the Supreme Soviet, the position of premier and of first secretary of the Party belong to the native domain and seem to be designed to convince the native Moslem population (as well as foreign public opinion) of the reality of autonomy supposedly enjoyed by the Union Republics.[11] The Uzbek prime minister was generally assisted by three or more vice-premiers of Russian and Uzbek nationality.[12] Between 1941 and 1946 most of the ministerial positions have been held by Moslems, while State Security was consistently headed by Europeans.[13] The position of foreign-affairs minister, upon its creation in 1944, was also logically assigned to an Uzbek. He did not establish any contact with foreign countries and remained a purely decorative figure. The newly created position of defense minister was never filled —not only in Uzbekistan, but in all other Union Republics as well.[14] The first Uzbek minister of foreign affairs in Soviet history was later rewarded for his "activity" (or rather, his inactivity) with a promotion to the position of a deputy chief of the Organization-Instruction Department in the Uzbek Central Committee's Secretariat —a function of higher responsibility than that of a minister in a republic like Uzbekistan.[15]

Several European deputies assisted the Moslem minister of agriculture, each in charge of specific operations.[16] In emergency cases the Russians' adjuncts were able to act not only behind the scenes, but openly and on their own. Thus the important decree prohibiting the collective farms and their members from selling grain before fulfilling the state grain-delivery quotas (1943) was signed by the Russian deputy chairman of the Council of People's Commissars and not by his Uzbek superior.[17]

The proportion of Moslem ministers in the Uzbek Council of Ministers amounted to four-fifths of the total, making its national composition the reverse of that of the Party secretariat. However, every ministry was controlled by a corresponding department of the secretariat. Thus native Moslem ministers, in addition to being assisted by Russian deputies, were placed under the supervision of the corresponding department chiefs of the Central Committee's secretariat, who most often happened to be Europeans. In the case of heavy industry the role of the Russian department chiefs appears even more prominent, because of the lack of corresponding ministerial positions in Tashkent.

Thus certain essential branches of economic activity were excluded from the local governmental jurisdiction, but nevertheless remained within the reach of the Uzbek Party secretariat. (See Table 6.) There, however, the role of the secretariat was not primarily to control. It was rather to secure the cooperation of local authorities for the operation of important factories established in, or evacuated into, Uzbekistan.

The movement of personnel between the Party secretariat, the Council of Ministers and the regional Party and Soviet organs was frequent. Officials were easily shifted from governmental to Party positions and vice versa, since all the officials were drawn from the same Party lists.

Three directions can be distinguished in the movement

Table 6

ECONOMIC DEPARTMENTS OF THE UZBEK CENTRAL
COMMITTEE'S SECRETARIAT AND THE CORRESPONDING
MINISTRIES IN UZBEKISTAN DURING THE 1940's

Supervising Department of the Secretariat	Supervised Ministry
Heavy industry and power:	
Industry*	no equivalent ministry in Tashkent; direct control by the federal ministries in Moscow.
Chemical industry*	
Electric power stations*	
Power and fuel*	
Transportation and communication*	— Highway transportation[b]
Consumer goods:	
Building and building materials[a]	Building materials Timber industry
Food,[c] textile and light industries	Textile industry Light industry[b] Flavoring-substances industry Food industry Meat and dairy industry
Trade and public catering*	— Commerce[d]
Local industry*	Local industry* Communal economy
Agriculture:	
Agriculture*	Agriculture Irrigation*
Cattle breeding	— Cattle breeding
State farms*	— State farms

SOURCE: *Pravda Vostoka* (Tashkent), 1941–46.

* European heads or ministers, 1941–46.
a European heads since 1944.
b European minister since 1943.
c Until 1943 separate department with a European chief.
d Native minister since 1943.

of Party personnel: demotion, promotion, and transfer on the same level. In the case of a demotion the name of the person involved was very often no longer mentioned, since demotion often meant jail. A promotion, on the other hand, could occur within the same organization or involve a transfer to another area or field of activity. We may assume that the general tendency of rotating Party officials from one job to another or from one region to another was motivated by the desire to prevent them from acquiring strong local connections which might lead to corruption and nepotism. After following the careers of numerous Party officials, it seems clear that while native Moslem officials were easily promoted, many Russian officials were usually shifted between key positions on the same level. The native Party official's career was almost always confined to his native region, while Russians and other Europeans were often shifted not only from one region to another, but from one Soviet republic to another.

The career of Mikhail Baskakov, who was appointed Uzbek minister of state security in 1946, is characteristic. Here are the jobs he held during twenty years, from 1938 to 1958:

1938–1943	Karelo-Finnish people's commissar of State Security
1943–?	Chief of administration, USSR people's commissariat of State Security
1946–1950	Uzbek minister of State Security
1950–?	Head, State Security for the Khabarovsk territory (Russian Republic)
1952–1958	Byelorussian minister of State Security.[18]

It is possible that some kind of "colonial pool" existed in Moscow from which Russian, Ukrainian, Georgian and other officials specialized in "colonial administration" were drawn for top Party assignments in Soviet Central Asia.

These trusted men constituted the nucleus on which the central Party organs of the Union Republic could rely, and the local Party members could be rallied. The existing situation was correctly described by a Turkestani émigré publication, which, at the same time, wrongly tends to exonerate native Communist officials from any responsibility for Soviet policy in Central Asia:

> The majority of Soviet ministers in Turkestan are Turkestanians, whereas the deputy ministers are Russian. The "ministers" are in fact Turkestanians who have been appointed as puppets while the real work is done by their "deputies". . . . The puppet ministers selected by Moscow amongst Turkestanian population have no power to take any independent administrative steps. . . .
>
> It would not therefore be right to make the Turkestanian ministers responsible for the Soviet Russian policies which are enforced in Turkestan. They are after all no more than the temporary servants of Moscow and so far from policy making are governed by the policy of the Soviet Union. Whilst the minister is thus no more than an executive, the actual decisions of policy are taken by the Central Committee of the Party. It is thus that the situation arises that the secretary of the Communist Party of a Soviet Republic has more powers than the State President or the Prime Minister himself. Correspondingly a head of department of the Party for some special subject has more right of action than a minister. With this whole network of official supervision the Turkestanian minister cannot do otherwise than to bow to Moscow orders.[19]

The 1950's

The policy of assigning European deputies to native ministers was still fully maintained in the 1950's. Despite the native majority in the Council of Ministers (sixteen out of twenty-one in 1955),[20] several of the more important ministerial positions were held by Europeans in

1957–58. The minister of irrigation (a very important position in Uzbekistan, where irrigation is essential to farming) was an old Russian bureaucrat, who had been third secretary of the Uzbek Communist Party during wartime. The minister of Communications, the minister of Highway Transportation, the head of the Committee of State Security (formerly minister of State Security) and the head of the militia (police) in the ministry of Interior were, as usual, Russians.[21]

Such a situation was not exclusive to Uzbekistan. According to Bennigsen, Russians, in 1957 were still in charge of political police (state-security apparatus) and communications in all the five Central Asian republics, of state planning in three out of five, and of local industry in four out of five.[22]

The Regional Party Apparatus

Structure

In speaking about the Party structure of a Union Republic, one usually refers to the highest level only, but for the mass of Soviet citizens their own local Party committee has been for many years of more direct importance than the powerful, but remote, higher Party authorities in the capital city.

The local Party organs are not just a "political machine" established in order to maintain Communist faith and prepare the traditional Soviet 99.9 per cent electoral majorities for the elections. Hundreds of positions in the district and thousands in a region (among the best-paid in the given area) cannot be obtained without their approval.[23] And, "because the road to power and to material privileges is open only through 'devotion' to the party . . . ,"[24] this patronage is indispensable to every career-minded individual. The Party Committee's authority covers almost every field. It is "accountable for the plan-fulfillment by all the economic enterprises of its region, and must consequently keep in touch with the entire economic life of the area and exert constant pressure on factories and collective farms to achieve and surpass the goals that have been set for them."[25] In regard to the many practical problems that Soviet citizens face, the Regional Party Committee acts as the authority entitled to hand down final verdicts. As on the higher levels, its everyday work is not carried on by the entire committee, but by its secretariat or by its bureau. Since the late 1930's the secretariat of a typical Regional Party Committee consisted of secretaries and of department chiefs; the bureau looked like an enlarged secretariat and included, in addition to the above, the chairman of the Executive Committee of the Regional Soviet (*Oblispolkom*), the first secretary of the regional Young Communist League (*Komsomol*), the editor of the regional newspaper and the heads of the state-security troops and of the military forces in the region.[26] The structure of the regional Party secretariat has been subject to a number of changes, mostly abolishing and restoring the economic departments, unifying or dividing certain departments, and changing the number of secretaries in the bureau (similar structural changes were made many times in Moscow). These changes were generally motivated by the practical necessities of the given time period and by the changing administrative practices of those in command. The prevailing structure of a Regional Party Committee in Uzbekistan in the 1940's is shown in Table 7.

In some regions, additional departments were established, while in rural areas the Industry Department was missing. The above-described Party machinery was designed to lead, advise and control the governmental apparatus, not supplant it. However, local governmental authorities were often driven into passivity by their Party counterparts, and tried to cover themselves by passing the burden of responsibility to higher authorities.[27] The cause of this state of affairs was evident: the local governmental personnel were hired and fired according to the Party's recommendations. Even the dates of meetings of the Executive Committees of the Regional Soviets was set up not by themselves, but by the Regional Party Committees. Important decrees were normally issued jointly. The passivity of local governmental authorities was thus self-explanatory.

It appears that some positions in the Regional Party Committees were usually in the hands of Europeans, while other positions always remained in the hands of the natives. After comparing the material collected on all nine regions of Uzbekistan, not much doubt remains concerning the pre-arranged character of this national setup. In general, Russians, Ukrainians, or Georgians were in charge of the majority of economic departments, of the Organization-Instruction Department and of the Special Sections. The positions of the second secretary also belonged to the European domain, and this was still true in 1956–58.[28] Natives, on the other hand, were in charge of propaganda and agitation, cadres' administration, work among women and of a minority of economic departments. The first secretary was generally a native.[29]

Certain legitimate doubts may be voiced about the possible implications of this state of affairs. It is often accepted that the first Party secretary is, "on the small scale, God and Tsar in the Region."[30] Does this mean that, in this case, the native first secretary is in full control, overshadowing his Russian colleagues? And in addition, could the control of the cadres' administration by the natives also be interpreted as a sign of their control of the local Party apparatus?

The answer to the first question might be found through

checking wartime Party careers of the officials concerned. Among the six successive second Party secretaries in the Samarkand region (all Europeans), three were promoted to the Uzbek Central Committee's secretariat. Two of them had already served as a second secretary in another region. At the same time, none of the three successive native first secretaries in Samarkand had a comparable Party record or seniority. One of them (Nasyr Makhmudov) entered the Party at the age of twenty-seven and became chairman of the Executive Committee of the Regional Soviet the same year (1940). Three years later he was given the job of first Party secretary.[31] The situation in Samarkand was not an exception. The same was true in the other regions of Uzbekistan.

The importance of the second secretary in non-Russian areas is being increasingly accepted even by those students of Soviet affairs who are not directly concerned with nationality problems. Thus Derek Scott from the University of Manchester acknowledges that ". . . for most non-Russian first secretaries there seems to be a Russian in the almost equally powerful office of second secretary."[32] A French expert on Central Asia, Helene Carrere d'Encausse, goes even further, stating that in non-Russian areas the position of second secretary is the more important one.[33] A British scholar on Soviet affairs, Hugh Seton-Watson, assumes that since the postwar purges in Central Asia mostly affected the Russian second secretaries, the real power was in their hands.[34]

At the departmental level, the department of Cadres' Administration during the war was mostly concerned with the mobilization and replacement of Party members in managerial and Party positions and of non-Party executives and technicians.[35] The power of the native secretary for Cadres' Administration was restricted by the role

Table 7

THE PREVAILING STRUCTURE OF REGIONAL PARTY COMMITTEES IN UZBEKISTAN DURING THE 1940's*

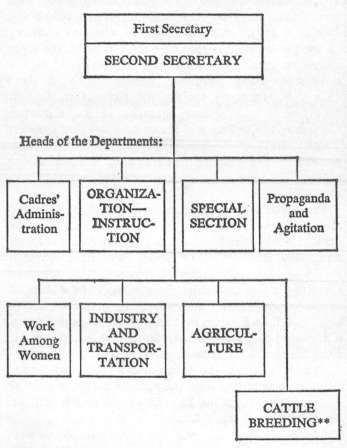

SOURCE: *Pravda Vostoka* (Tashkent).

* Departments generally headed by Europeans (Russians, Ukrainians, Byelorussians, Georgians, Armenians, European Jews, etc.) are indicated in capital letters.

** Russians were as frequently in charge of the cattle-breeding department as the natives.

played by his European deputy and especially by the importance of the European chief of the Special Section who was responsible for the political reliability of local Party cadres. The native secretaries of Propaganda and Agitation were strictly secondary figures. In some regions they were even temporarily assigned to look after farming, causing them to neglect their own duties.[36]

The Organization-Instruction Department (now Department of Party Organs), a European stronghold in the 1940's as well as in the 1950's, played a first-hand role in the regional Party structure. Besides supervising the work of lower Party organizations, it functioned as a channel for central bureaucratic directives and was the main controller of the fulfillment of Party directives.[37] Ever since Stalin's rise to power the efforts of this department had been directed toward "the elimination of opposition in the localities and the transformation of the Party bureaucracy into a solid support for the General Secretary."[38]

Among the grass-roots Party membership in Uzbekistan, Europeans supposedly accounted for 51 per cent shortly before World War II.[39] Just before the war started, only 57.5 per cent of the secretaries of the primary Party organizations in Uzbekistan were natives. Only half had a complete high-school education or more, and 92 per cent had less than three years of Party experience. The second figure can be easily explained by the fact that only three years had then elapsed since the end of the "Great Purge." The new cadres were probably still very inexperienced, since the work of 80.9 per cent of all the primary Party organizations in Uzbekistan was judged unsatisfactory.[40] The exact proportion of Europeans among the Party members in Uzbekistan in the 1950's is unknown. Carrere d'Encausse and Bennigsen acknowledge their ignorance of this matter. Monteil gives us the following figures: 40 per cent in 1952 and 31 per cent in 1954,[41] but his sources are unknown.

It could be argued that the continued shortage of competent native cadres compelled the Party to use the services of better-qualified Europeans. This would not explain, however, why Europeans were assigned to certain specific branches, leaving other positions to native Communists. Moreover, Europeans were instructed to help native cadres carry out Party tasks. They were also supposed to keep the native Communists under control and to prevent the development of nationalist and separatist tendencies among them. They were the frame, and without them the local native Party structure could not have survived.

Activity

The main activities of the Regional Party Committee may be broken up into the day-to-day work routine of the secretariat, sessions of the bureau and conferences.

The bureau of the Regional Party Committee had its own work schedules and was in session each 8–9 days. The work of each session revolved around an agenda of up to one hundred items. The number of people attending closed sessions varied according to the problems discussed. In addition to the bureau members, Party instructors, district secretaries, collective-farm chairmen and factory directors were often invited to attend. It was widely known that any Soviet official, manager, or director could at any time be summoned to such a session for questioning or admonition. "The summons to appear before the Bureau frequently signified trouble, but this was not invariably the rule,"[42] wrote Professor Fainsod about the Smolensk region of Russia in the 1930's, and this statement is still not outdated. The bureau was concerned with all the Party matters and with the state of affairs in the subordinate Party organizations. A great deal of attention was given to the problem of Party cadres—appointments, removals, shifts of personnel. Economic problems—sewing, harvesting, fulfilling state delivery quotas in agriculture—and plan fulfillment in industry were of great concern.

Officially, the daily work routine was divided between the political and the economic departments, each department having its own work planned according to a special schedule. In practice, however, the political departments were always deeply concerned with economic matters. Thus the Uzbek Republican Conference on Propaganda and Agitation of December, 1944 (attended by the secretaries for Propaganda and Agitation from all the regions and districts of the republic), turned solely on the problem of increasing cotton production. A similar conference in March, 1946, placed a like emphasis on the same problem.[43]

There were good reasons why this overlapping continued. Policy making had always been outside the Regional Party Committee domain. There had never been an attempt at this level to develop fresh ideas in the field of Marxist-Leninist theory. The large majority of Party members was not even prepared to discuss those ideas which became part of the official Party dogma.[44] Political education in Uzbekistan, as in the other parts of the Soviet Union, was based mainly on the limited wisdom of Stalin's *Kratkii Kurs* (short course of the history of the Communist Party of the Soviet Union).[45] The iron rules of Stalinist discipline and conformity were strictly enforced. Under the pretense of maintaining Party unity, not much room was left for genuine "non-guided" discussion.

Excluded from decision making (even in regard to problems of Union Republic concern), the Regional

Party Committee directed its energy toward fulfilling the goals fixed for its region from above. This task, especially during the war period, was reduced to one main purpose —*to get things done* in industry and farming. As a result of this, the bureau of the Regional Party Committee functioned as some kind of giant managerial board, empowered by the owner (the state) to supervise the economy of the region in its own name. "There were times when the *Obkom* Bureau appeared almost indistinguishable from the Commissariat of Agriculture,"[46] writes Professor Fainsod about Smolensk in the 1930's. Reading *Pravda Vostoka* reports of all the conferences and meetings held by the Regional Party Committee in Samarkand during the years 1941–1946, the picture appears identical, if not even more extreme.[47] The wartime burden of economic responsibility was by no means easy. Moscow was setting heavy agricultural delivery quotas for every Central Asian republic. The latter, in turn, were distributing their quotas among the regions. The regional authorities, in their turn, were dividing the burden among the districts, and the district authorities were finally fixing the quota for each collective farm within their jurisdiction. The Tashkent papers were full of recriminations against the shortcomings of the regional leadership in the field of farming. The following titles of articles printed in *Pravda Vostoka* in 1943, 1944 and 1945 are characteristic of such high pressure on the Samarkand Party leadership: "Sugar Beet Sowing Ruined in Samarkand" (August 16, 1943), "Combine Harvesting Ruined in Samarkand" (July 9, 1944), "Summer Tractor Repairs Ruined in Samarkand" (August 12, 1944), "Tractor Repairs Ruined in Samarkand" (February 7, 1945), "They are Dragging Harvest and Grain Deliveries in Samarkand" (July 24, 1945), "Precious Time Lost in Samarkand. Cotton Harvest Menaced" (July 25, 1945).

Similar articles appeared every year concerning all fields

of agricultural activity in all the regions of Uzbekistan. Verbal pressure was not, however, the only means used. Strong measures were also taken in order to reach the production goals established for the region, regardless of sacrifice and hardships. The guilty ones were speedily removed. The failure of a spring sowing in the region was sufficient reason for the removal of the first Party secretary in Samarkand.[48] In the so-called "Andijan Case," a Russian first secretary was assigned to this cotton-rich region in order to expedite agricultural production. Because of the importance of the task, the native figurehead was, for the time, discarded. The new secretary used strong-arm methods—threat and punishment. Some of the collective-farm chairmen were brought to trial and received harsh sentences. The Andijan region was ahead in grain deliveries for a while, and the "Appeal of Andijan Collective Farmers" to the collective farmers of other regions to overfulfill grain-delivery quotas was often lauded in the press. As long as a satisfactory margin of achievement was maintained, no one challenged the new secretary's right to act the way he did. But after two years the cattle stock in the region had fallen by half, the average yield in agriculture by two-thirds. The Central Committee of the Communist Party in Moscow subsequently opened an inquiry and removed the man, accusing him of the same misdeeds they had tolerated before the failure of his program. The chairman of the Executive Committee of the Andijan Soviet (a native) was also removed.[49] The first secretary of the Central Committee of the Communist Party of Uzbekistan, pointing to the repressive methods used by the culprit, had to concede that:

> Certainly, there is nothing easier than to fire one or another functionary, to inflict a penalty upon him or to bring his case before the law. It is much more difficult . . . to overcome the obstacles in the work itself.[50]

Such wise ideas were unfortunately seldom put into action, and failures tended to be connected with the wrongdoing of a specific person or persons. Thus the Andijan Case did not bring about a radical change of methods, but merely another change of personalities. An assistant secretary in the Uzbek Central Committee's secretariat, also a European, was rushed to Andijan to take over the task and to repair the damage. Party meetings were held all over Uzbekistan to stress the "errors of the Andijan Party orgainzation" as an example to others. It does not mean, however, that the region started to perform miracles right after the wrong men had been removed from office. "The Andijan region is sharply falling behind in cotton cultivation," was the sad comment of one of the first articles in *Pravda Vostoka* during the 1945 cotton season.[51]

Unlike the first and second secretaries, responsible for the region as a whole, the chiefs of the economic departments had a more limited field of action. They guided and controlled the respective branches of economic activity entrusted to their supervision. Their interference, however, gave an additional headache to the hard-pressed industrial managers, who were already caught between a number of superiors, controllers and supervisors who were not always in agreement with each other—their own trust or ministry, the financial agents of the State Bank and of the Financial Department, the inspectors of the Ministry of State Control, the delegates of Moscow's Ministry of Supply, the corresponding local governmental and Party authorities. A good department head needed great ability to maintain his authority without encroaching on the prerogatives of all the people involved in bureaucratic decision making. In addition, he was not always able to carry out his own decisions. Sometimes the decisions taken by him and approved by the bureau remained only on paper because of failure to control their execution.[52] Bureaucratic directives were obeyed when accompanied by control and enforcement, and, if not, the subordinate institution, blessed with one more instruction, directive or reminder, was inclined to brush it aside or to answer it with another piece of paper. A number of such instructions never went (often fortunately, sometimes unfortunately) beyond the filing cabinets.

In addition to the control exercised by the economic branch departments, the Regional Party Committee sometimes assigned several of its members to an area of critical shortcomings—to supervise, for example, the progress of the agricultural campaign in a specific district.[53] Such a group constituted a real whip over the District Party Committee and prevented it from shielding the interest of its district against pressure from above.

Party conferences and plenums, which took place at least once a year, followed a standard pattern: conferences consisted of a report delivered by the first or the second secretary of the Regional Party Committee, or, in very important cases, by the representative of the Central Committee of the Communist Party of Uzbekistan himself, who was always present. In the case of Samarkand it was the Russian second secretary of the Central Committee of the Communist Party of Uzbekistan who was generally assigned to this task.[54] The same was true in the late 1950's. The report was always followed by debates, with the district Party secretaries and managers of industrial, commercial, and agricultural enterprises taking part. The subjects of the reports were always identical with those previously debated at the higher level. The only difference between the conferences' agendas from one region to another was in administrative questions (mainly concerned with shifting officials within the Party apparatus). Usually present, too, were the chiefs of the regional state security forces, the head of the regional police (militia), and the military commissar. On one occasion, the general in command of the Turkestan Military Territory attended.[55] The resolutions adopted on the higher level were always approved and their fulfillment solemnly pledged.

In addition to regular conferences and plenums, the Regional Party Committee organized a number of economic and specialized conferences and meetings, like the "collective-farm elite" conference, a cotton-growing rally, a meeting of the "Party elite," a meeting of the Party managerial elite, a conference of the district chiefs of Organization-Instruction Departments, a conference of secretaries for propaganda and agitation, etc.[56] Some of the more important meetings were also attended by a secretary of the Uzbek Central Committee. Typical was the Interdistrict grain conference in Samarkand in July, 1942. It was attended by the Party secretaries of the major grain-producing districts, by the chiefs of the political departments of the state farms and other officials. The Russian third secretary of the Central Committee of the Communist Party of Uzbekistan was sent from Tashkent to deliver the main speech.[57]

The largest factories in the republic, from among those working for defense, were given the name of "factories of all-Union importance" and placed in a position of relative independence from local Party authorities. The latter were prevented from interfering with the orders of their managers, who were controlled directly by Moscow. Special Party organizers of Moscow's Central Committee directly responsible to Moscow were in charge of their Party organization. They enjoyed an unusually high "prestige" among the workers. The Tashkent press reported that the paper of one of these factories was printing letters from workers beginning with "Due to your true Bolshevik solicitude," or "In response to your thoughtfulness," and addressed to the director and the Party organizer.[58] According to recent Soviet data, only eighteen factories in Uzbekistan were granted such distinction.[59] These were exceptional cases. For the most part, the Regional Party Committee remained the real master of the political and economic life of the whole region. The only persons able to challenge its authority were the military commissar and the chief of the regional state security forces, but only in their respective fields.

The Local Party Apparatus: District and City Level

Much of the regional structure was duplicated in the district setup. The bureau of the District Party Committee was patterned on that of the Regional Party Committee. All the district officialdom, from the first secretary down to the MTS and state-farm directors, was subjected to regional Party approval. The election of district and city Party officials follows the general pattern of Soviet elections at every level. A candidate is "suggested" from the top levels. His name is then presented to the meeting by somebody from the ranks and "unanimously" approved. The Communist Party strove, however, to preserve at least the appearance of inner Party democracy. Thus the instances where elections were brushed aside as a formality and replaced by open "co-optation" were always condemned.[60]

While relatively little was written abroad about the district level of Party hierarchy in general, the district structure in Uzbekistan is even less known. Foreign tourists, among the small number of persons visiting Central Asia, seldom spend more than a few hours in district centers. Soviet district newspapers are unavailable outside Russia. Sporadic coverage in Tashkent papers and personal reminiscences of people who lived there (mostly during World War II) are the only sources of information available. The following study covers all the districts of the Samarkand region. One of the districts (Zaamin) is given particular attention. The newspaper dates were checked against the personal experience of those familiar with that area. Despite obvious limitations, these two sources shed some light on the subject. It becomes clear that the national distribution of key positions at the district level follows the regional pattern. While there are not enough data concerning the chiefs of the Organization-Instruction Departments and Special Sections, the pattern of European second secretaries, characteristic of the regional party structures, was clearly maintained. Out of twenty-one districts of the Samarkand region, seven had a European second secretary most of the time and one a European first secretary during the crucial war years. Data on eight are lacking. Only two districts of less importance had native secretaries in both. The three main districts of the Samarkand region followed the same pattern. At the city level, among the three cities of the region (Samarkand, Dzhizak and Katta-Kurgan), European control was even stronger. In Samarkand from 1943 to 1946 even the position of the first secretary passed into European hands. The necessity for getting things done prevailed over the desire to appease native sensibility. In Katta-Kurgan, for example, both the first secretary and the chief of the Organization-Instruction Department were Europeans. Dzhizak presumably followed a similar pattern. In the urban districts of the Samarkand City (Old Native City, New Russian City and Railroad district, mostly Russian) only the first Party secretary of the Old City was a native Moslem.[61]

Tashkent, the capital of the Uzbek Republic, presented an extreme picture of Russian domination. Except for the Cadres' Administration secretary and second secretary, no important position and only a few secondary ones were held by Uzbeks in the Tashkent City Party Committee during the war years. All the successive first secretaries, as well as half of the successive second secretaries, were Europeans. Europeans were also in charge of organization-instruction, transportation, power and fuel, armaments (most of the time), propaganda and agitation and of light and textile industry as well.[62] It is, again, an illustration of the priority given to performance over local political considerations.

The Regional Party Committee maintained a close watch over the activities of the District Party Committee, keeping the latter under constant pressure, supervision and control. District authorities were submerged by a continuous flow of instructions dealing with all possible topics, even seemingly unimportant ones, and had to present reports indicating fulfillment of regional directives in Party work, farming and in many other fields. Periodic checkups by regional officials held the district officials up to schedule.

In some cases the whip over the district was manned by a more powerful authority than the Regional Party Committee—the Uzbek Central Committee itself. Decisions taken in Tashkent were written in denunciatory language full of such phrases as "pointing out," "warning," "making responsible," "entrusting with," "giving the notice," "switching over the responsibility." At the district level the efficient work of the Executive Committee of the District Soviet, and especially of its agriculture department, were indispensable to the control of grain deliveries. In order to preserve their efficiency, regional authorities intervened sometimes to protect the latter from the more powerful District Party Committee. But the nullification of the authority of the Soviet reached, in some cases, such proportions that it brought criticism from the Tashkent press:

The District Party Committees instead of helping the Executive Committee of the District Soviet often take over its tasks. . . .

The leading officials of the latter, on the other hand, are used to the idea that their job consists in signing joint resolutions and in avoiding initiative; they do not attempt to face any of the problems independently. . . .

It is not unexpected therefore that few of the kolkhoz presidents turn to the latter to solve their problems. They prefer to apply directly to the Party Committee.[63]

The District Party Committee not only gave advice and solved problems, it also appointed chairmen of collective farms without regard for the opinion of its members of the respective farms. Constant violations of the collective-farm charter were commonly accepted. The customary way of handling the elections of collective-farm chairmen by district officials was described in one of the *Pravda Vostoka* articles. In that case, the district authority was represented by the chairman of the head of the Executive Committee of the District Soviet. He arrived at the meeting of the collective-farm Soviet while the chairman of the farm was in the hospital. He told those present to elect as a new chairman a protégé of his, a man with a poor reputation, little known to the farmers. "Who is against?" he asked. "Nobody?" Then so and so is "unanimously elected as the new chairman." Another official of the collective farm tried to protest by saying that "we already have a chairman," but he was swiftly silenced, "unanimously" voted out of office and finally ordered under arrest.

The new chairman lived up to his reputation: he immediately sold twenty-three lambs and pocketed the money. Then he silenced the protesting farmers by threatening them. The regional authorities, as well as the Ministry of Agriculture, were aware of the goings on, but nothing was done against those abuses, complains the article.[64] What matters, however, is not the fact that an embezzler was forced upon the collective farm by the authorities, but rather that the farmers, no matter how they felt, had no voice in the selection of their own chairman. The fact is that the elections with their "who is for," "who is against" and "who abstains" were a sheer formality. In this particular case, after the "candidate" failed at first to receive the necessary majority, the district official duly scolded the audience and proceeded with another vote.

The removal procedure was even simpler. At the meeting of the bureau of the District Party Committee, the Party secretary had to put forth the motion for the removal of the collective-farm chairman he wished to fire. The collective farm involved did not even have to be consulted.[65] Such practice, according to known first-hand reports and to Professor Fainsod's findings from the Smolensk archives, was not exceptional. This was the rule of Soviet life, and the reverse was rather the exception. District Party and Soviet officials became accustomed to interfering constantly in the affairs of collective farms. Only extreme cases involving severe damages to farm property were criticized by the press. *Pravda Vostoka* characterized the native first secretary of the Ak-Darya district as a man "who is not against appropriating collective farm goods for himself" and whose brother was a rogue. Nevertheless, he remained in office until the end of the war and possibly longer.

In another case, it was brought to the attention of regional Party authorities that self-appropriations of collective farm land were made in the same district by another local Party official and by some Soviet managers. A similar misuse of power prevailed in regard to the

Machine-Tractor Stations (MTS). The orders of MTS directors were sometimes rescinded by local Party secretaries.[66] District Party authorities relied on the MTS directors for a number of activities, often unrelated to their direct functions. This passing of the responsibility from the higher to the lower rungs of the ladder was common in the Party affairs.

Some District Party secretaries went to another extreme: unable to cope with the pressure of everyday work, they practically lost control over the work of various District Party Committee departments. Sometimes such a state of affairs led to a situation in which local managers and technicians proceeded on their own, paying only token attention to the bureaucratic directives issued by the Party Committee. In some other cases Party secretaries were just unwilling to get their boots dirty by visiting the farms, and preferred to direct the collective farm's activity from the comfortable chairs of their city offices.[67]

Firing of unfit Party officials was widespread. A conference of district Cadres' Administration officials of the Samarkand region (summer, 1945) revealed that during the first five months of 1945, 22 per cent of city and district Party officials of the region had been replaced. In particular districts over one-half of the leading Party bureaucrats had been fired.[68] Such a high turnover rate was not improving the efficiency of the Party work.

Party interference in industry was just as pronounced as in agriculture. Speaking about the Party's guidance of industry, a Party instructor stated that:

Administration by mere injunction, intimidation, interference with operative management is, unfortunately, the "style" of leadership of the Samarkand Party officials over the factory managers. . . .

The District Party secretary intimidated factory directors

and threatened them with expulsion from Party and job as well as with legal action.[69]

A factory's Party organizer, unlike a Party secretary, was not in a position to intimidate a Communist director, himself a member of the Party elite. Thus in a factory of a textile trust in Namagan, the director managed to oust three Party organizers one after another. The City Party Committee upheld the director's stand.[70]

Requests for goods and services from Party officials for themselves and their protégés were as frequent as their threats. When money became available to the housing authority in Samarkand, the Party officials were the first to be served, exhausting all the available funds.[71] In another instance a curious note was written by a Samarkand Party official to a factory director:

In connection with the departure of the [Party] lecturer, who was conducting his lectures on a high politico-ideological level, we request that you supply him with five cans of food.[72]

Party officials were far from being tolerant to critics. Instances are known where rural correspondents have been persecuted by Party secretaries annoyed by their critical remarks.[73]

Party members in good standing with the District Party Committee were in most cases assured of good jobs, regardless of their qualifications. Some exaggerated cases were chastised by the press, but they were by no means exceptional. For example, a Moslem Party member in Bukhara held, during his rather short Party career, the following positions: secretary of the city organization of the Young Communist League, deputy political head of the militia, director of a bathing establishment, manager of a commercial trust, deputy director of an MTS, director of the "Cooperative Union of the Toilers of the Orient," head of the regional department of fine arts and instructor of the Executive Committee of the Regional Soviet. Another native Communist was a stock-clerk's helper, president of a builder's committee, secretary of an MTS and director of a technical college. Such "versatile" men were on hand to fill all possible vacancies. For this very purpose the Party Committees held special "lists of candidates for responsible positions" called "District Party Reserves."[74] It goes without saying that many of these candidates were totally unfit for their prospective jobs and could not remain in office without endangering the operation of the enterprise they were supposed to manage. Examples are given of factory directors who had no idea about salaries and other basic economic facts.[75] Some native directors had to ask their Russian subordinates to write the reports that they were to deliver at the next Party meeting. This situation led to an abnormally high turnover of Soviet management personnel.

The conduct of the inner Party work was a duty of the District Party Committee. The latter was responsible for the work of primary Party and Communist Youth organizations, for the recruitment, admission, education, and expulsion of Party members and for political propaganda and agitation in general. District Party secretaries were, however, much too busy with the local economy to pay much attention to these problems. As Professor Fainsod states: "The *Raikom* meeting often read like an agriculture calendar."[76] Thus the handing over of all Party work to the Organization-Instruction Departments became a usual practice in many of the District Party Committees. In one of the districts of the Tashkent region, for example, the Organization-Instruction Department worked out a "plan of holding the elections." It was stated by the press that this was primarily the duty of the first and second district secretaries, and not of the Organization-Instruction

Department.[77] The registration of transfers and of new
Party members, a duty of the district secretary, was sometimes conveniently passed to the head of the Party statistics
sector. At times, pressure for grain deliveries, plan fulfillment, keeping up with production, sowing, harvesting and
tractor-repair schedules, and other administrative necessities reduced the political activity of the local Party
apparatus to an almost complete standstill.

The neglect of political activity, especially of Marxist-
Leninist theory, prevailed even at the most responsible
Party levels. Party secretaries, local Soviet officials and
even ministers in Tashkent were criticized for indifference
to Marxist-Leninist theory.[78] Nor is this surprising. An
American author explains the situation as follows:

Due to a shortage of trained leaders . . . it was impossible
to regulate closely entrance into the Party. As a consequence,
there grew up an amorphous, undisciplined group of self-
styled communists, many of whom entered the Party to promote their own selfish ends and almost none of whom had
ever heard of Karl Marx.[79]

The shortage of qualified candidates, critical in the
1920's, was still very much evident in the early 1940's.
The newspapers criticized the habit of some district Party
officials in recommending "unfit people" for Party membership. "The taste for theoretical studies is gone," com-
plained *Pravda Vostoka,* blaming several secretaries and
other Party officials of the Samarkand region for indifference to Communist theory. Nor was this exceptional. In
many districts attendance in the school for the Party
elite was poor. Many district officials were semiliterate.
In the Samarkand region, among the twenty-eight groups
of lecturers projected to work in rural areas during the
summer of 1946, only seven actually worked, and these
poorly.[80] A Party secretary who was often seen inspecting

the progress of the sowing or harvesting in the collective farms seldom paid any attention to political work in the same farms. Newspapers reached one of the remote districts of the Samarkand region from ten to fifteen days after the date of their publication, and no political lecturers had visited the *raion* for over a year. The chief of the Organization-Instruction Department and other district officials were politically ignorant.[81]

The district press, badly managed and discouraged by a general lack of interest, was afraid to print anything which could possibly be judged as unorthodox. It was always tempting to "play it safe" by copying articles from the regional newspapers. Plagiarism went so far that the Tashkent press chastised the Zaamin district newspaper *Kolkhoz Galabasy* for the habit of filling most of its columns with reprints from the regional newspaper *Leninsky Put*. Zaamin Party secretaries were blamed for their indifference to the situation. In the rural districts of the Kashka-Darya region in 1943, even the heads of the powerful Organization-Instruction Departments were sent to collective farms to raise production. As a consequence, Party meetings were almost forgotten, and in some of the districts new Party candidates were neither sought nor accepted.[82] But a genuine interest toward political matters could hardly be maintained, even with a less indifferent Party membership. For the local Party apparatus was transformed into some kind of economic caretaker, with Party policy and political matters confined to a much higher level.

Chapter 9

Conclusion

THE EFFECTIVENESS of the Soviet policy in Central Asia is indisputable. The nationalist Basmachi revolt was effectively crushed. Industrialization and collectivization programs were carried on. Cultural and social revolutions were accomplished. During all the difficult years, and despite all the hardships imposed upon the peoples of Central Asia by the rapid transformation of life, the internal situation never got out of hand after the beginning of the 1930's. It is true that many Soviet measures encountered a good amount of coolness, indifference and even bad will, but the local native population never actively opposed nor openly protested against them.[1] This was especially remarkable in wartime, when it was necessary to drop some of the window-dressing devices usually hiding the reality of Russian control.

One should remember, however, that colonial peoples in French and British possessions showed signs of unrest only after having seen and experienced the weakening of their respective colonial masters during World War II. The increasing strength of Russia's position in world affairs was certainly not the right kind of invitation for the peoples of Central Asia to challenge Russia's domination. Thus Russia was able to carry out its policy throughout the vicissitudes of war without the slightest surrender of her privileges.

The double-standard policy of advocating self-determination for British, French and other nations' possessions, but denying the same to its own, has quite old and prosaic roots. Already in 1922 Zinoviev, then prominent in Soviet government, affirmed that although Russia had renounced the policy of exploitation of her dependencies,

. . . we cannot do without the petroleum of Azerbaijan or the cotton of Turkestan. We take these products which are necessary for us not as the former exploiters, but as older brothers bearing the torch of civilization.[2]

Soviet scholars show righteous indignation about bourgeois "pseudo-scholars who try to whitewash and embellish" the colonial policies of their respective countries.[3] There are, however, in Central Asia several administrative patterns strongly reminiscent of the very same. The first one is the military control of the area by Russian troops. Because of the system of shifting draftees from their places of residence to the other end of the country, a number of Russians and Ukrainians from the European part of the USSR or from Siberia serve in Central Asia, while most of the Turkestani Moslems serve far from their own land. The Turkestan military district has been built on the old tsarist pattern: Russian military garrisons are stationed in the principal cities and Russian generals are in command, even after Stalin's death.[4] Such an arrangement has the familiar flavor of the traditional "colonialist" pattern of keeping "native troops" out of their own land and controlling a dependent area by metropolitan troops, or by soldiers from a different dependency.

The second pattern of "colonial administration" consists in the fact that the Soviet security apparatus in Central Asia, besides its usual police occupations, is also entrusted with the task of preventing and suppressing nationalist "chauvinist" tendencies among the native Moslem population. For this reason natives have seldom been included in the top positions of the security network. Thus, in wartime Uzbekistan, the offices of the minister of State Security and of the heads of Special Sections in the Central Committee's secretariat and in the Regional Party Committees were held by Russians and other Europeans.[5] Heads of regional State Security units were also Europeans. Nor has this pattern been restricted to wartime Uzbekistan. Throughout the 1950's the ministers of State Security in all five Central Asian Republics were Russians or Ukrainians; none was a Moslem.[6]

The third and most important feature is the Communist Party apparatus itself, the dominant force in every area of Soviet political, administrative, social and economic life. Identical in leadership and doctrine from Leningrad to Samarkand, moving toward the same goals all over the USSR, the Party is the only active force capable of providing an ideological justification for "teaching . . . the small Uzbek cotton grower . . . the ideals of the Leningrad worker." Remove the shield of Communist ideology, and there is little difference between Russia's relationship with her Central Asian possessions and that of England and France with their dependencies in the past. This is why the degree of Russian control over local Party organizations, the degree of trust shown to Party members and officials of local nationalities, the distribution of key positions in the leading Party organs between Moslem and Russian officials, and a number of similar patterns present such an interesting picture.

The pattern of assigning responsible Party positions within the local apparatus to outsiders was fully applied in the western Ukraine after its annexation by the USSR in 1939.[7] These measures were reintroduced after the liberation of the area from German occupation, although local people were then given more prominence in the state apparatus.[8] The connection between this approach and the idea of unreliability of local western Ukrainian cadres is obvious. The persistence of similar patterns in an area such as Central Asia, Soviet since the Revolution but Moslem and Turkic in culture, is revealing and places the Soviet policy in Central Asia uncomfortably close to the old and familiar colonial policies.

Recent Khrushchev moves toward decentralization of industry and the downgrading of Stalin and of some of his practices were mistakenly viewed by many native Party officials as a sign of Moscow's retreat from the "colonial pattern" in the distribution of offices. Such premature expectations were condemned during the June 23–26, 1959, session of the Academy of Science devoted to the problems of building of Communism in the USSR:

National cadres can and should always work in Moscow and in other cities of Russia, exactly as Russians and representatives of other [non-native] nationalities can and should work in the national republics.[9]

The Soviet regime, aware of the spiritual link existing between Moslem peoples at home and abroad,[10] has found itself, in dealing with Islam, hesitating between two political alternatives, each based on a different concept of the Communist Revolution.

One alternative reflected the views of Mir Said Sultan Oglu (known otherwise as Sultan Galiev) and called for extending the revolution into the colonial countries, especially among Moslems. According to his views, this colonial revolution, appealing to all social classes of the colonial peoples, would bring about the collapse of the capitalist-colonialist West.[11] The approach assumed the use of Soviet Moslems in Moscow's propaganda campaigns directed toward neighboring Moslem countries, and favored interrelations between the Soviet Republics of Central Asia and their non-Communist neighbors.

The second alternative reflected the views of Joseph Stalin and called for an orthodox Marxist approach toward the problems of revolution in Asia. Connected with the initial weakness of the Soviet Union and with the "bourgeois nationalist" feelings still active in Central Asia, this approach resulted in the Soviet policy of severing relations between Soviet and foreign Moslems for the sake of isolating the former from Moslem, Pan-Turkic and Pan-Iranian influence. Such a policy, discarding the internationalist approach of early revolutionary days, was based upon the Soviet desire to consolidate "socialism in one country" and promote the policy of Russification in Central Asia.

Soviet studies of the non-Soviet Orient closely followed the shifting pattern of Soviet policies. Walter Z. Laqueur offers the following chronological division of such studies:

1919–28—friendly attitude toward Asian nationalist movements expressed in Soviet studies.
1929–34—hostility toward the same movements.
1935–37—revival of the initial attitude.
1938–48—events in Asia mostly ignored.
1948–54—slow revival of the friendly attitude.
1954 on —real revival of the friendly attitude.[12]

Despite the 1956 return to Sultan Galiev's position in foreign affairs, marked by a Soviet aid agreement to Moslem bourgeois-nationalist movements in the Middle East, the Islamic foundations of the Central Asian society remained, in Soviet eyes, a spiritual basis for anti-Communist and anti-Russian ideology. As stated by a Soviet specialist on Islam:

. . . it is necessary to pay much more attention to the unmasking of the contemporary role of Islam in the support of the exploiting classes and colonial regimes, to the disclosing of the reactionary content of the Pan-Islamic and Pan-Turkic ideologies used for the benefit of American imperialists in their goal of enslaving the peoples of the Orient.[13]

A 1958 Moscow broadcast by another specialist on Islam, Professor L. L. Klimovich, condemned the Moslem faith as "a remnant of the past which the Soviet people have left far behind," and assailed Moslem religious leaders as reactionaries and fanatical even in the Soviet republics of Central Asia.[14] According to an English author:

The presence of large numbers of Russian and Ukrainian settlers, who are hardworking and to a large extent free from *colon* prejudice, has contributed considerably to the development of industry and agriculture and thus to the material well-being of the native population. Indeed, it would be not unfair to say that the Soviet experiment in Central Asia and Transcaucasia is a good example of what a deliberate and determined policy of colonialism can achieve. But it is nonetheless colonialism, for there is no glimmer of those hopes of real independence which in other parts of Asia and in Africa have either come to fruition or have long been stirring.

And the same author added:

. . . there are certain circumstances which suggest that the absence of open opposition to the present regime springs more from resignation and fear than from real contentment.[15]

Another English visitor summarizes his impressions as follows:

The ultimate decision, the ultimate authority, the ultimate power rests with Moscow. The Party line comes from Moscow, the troops are under the command of Moscow. . . .[16]

The persistence and survival of Moslem Turkestani nationalism (sometimes called localism) is acknowledged by most of the leading Western experts in the field, including Bennigsen, Monteil, Kolarz, Caroe, Laqueur, Pipes, Carrere d'Encausse and many others, and denied only by openly pro-Communist authors like Tubert or Egretaud. The recent utilization of Soviet Central Asia as a showpiece for visitors from the newly independent underdeveloped countries of Asia and Africa tends to work both ways. While an African guest is admiring new Tashkent factories, his Uzbek host cannot help wondering why nationalism and self-determination are virtues abroad and sins at home.

Soviet publications show much interest in Western, especially American, research on Central Asia, and look with great displeasure upon those writers who do not accept their views on this matter. The first secretary of the Communist Party of Uzbekistan, Rashidov, recently wrote as follows:

> . . . Bourgeois scribblers for hire, with or without learned degrees, utilize the concoctions of various Hayits [Baymirza Hayit, a Turkestani émigré writer], Pipeses [Richard Pipes from Harvard], Douglases [Judge William O. Douglas] and Parks [Alexander G. Park from Columbia], furiously calumniate the Soviet reality, perverting the meaning of Leninist nationality policy and deny its success, trying to undermine in this way the sympathy of millions of ordinary people all over the world towards the Soviet country.[17]

Rashidov's remarks constitute additional proof of the necessity for serious and objective inquiries into various aspects of Communist nationality policies in Central Asia.

A long and painful evolution and liberalization of the Soviet policy is needed to advance the degree of autonomy of these Soviet republics of Central Asia, where the natives are still in the majority, even to the humble level enjoyed by such satellites as Bulgaria or Rumania. The possibility of such a change cannot, however, be totally discounted. Central Asia, located between Russian Siberia, China and the Moslem world, could easily become a cause of serious conflict among the three worlds. It is up to Soviet Russia to forestall this future threat by either accelerating its process of colonization of the territory by Russian settlers and of continuous cultural absorption of the natives, or by letting the Moslem peoples of Central Asia follow their own "road to socialism." The development of any sort of national Communism, even externally obedient to Moscow, is, however, still out of the question, for such a development would necessitate much more "liberalization" than the Kremlin seems at present prepared to grant.

Notes

(Two reference works cited in table footnotes and in chapter notes are abbreviated as follows: *Bolshaia Sovetskaia Entsiklopediia* as *BSE; Malaia Sovetskaia Entsiklopediia* as *MSE.*)

Chapter 1: Historical Background

1. This introductory chapter is based mostly on the historical material from V. I. Massalski, "Turkestanski Krai," *Rossiia, polnoe geograficheskoe opisanie nashego otechestva* (St. Petersburg: A. F. Davrien, 1913), Vol. 13. See also a small book by Mary Holdsworth, *Turkestan in the Nineteenth Century* (Oxford: Central Asian Research Center), 1959. For the pre-Russian period see W. Barthold, *Histoire des Turcs d'Asie Centrale* (Paris: Andrien-Maisonneuve), 1945.

2. While suppressing Kazakh revolts, the Russian government encouraged the Kazakhs in 1855 to capture and enslave the Bashkirs, who had fled to the steppe after the suppression of the Batyrsha revolt in Bashkiria.

3. The Samarkand-Tashkent-Andizhan section was built in 1895–99 and the Orenburg-Tashkent railroad in 1900–05.

4. N. V. Arkhipov, *Sredne-Aziatskie respubliki* (Moscow-Leningrad: Gosizdat, 1930), pp. 86–87.

5. G. Safarov, *Kolonialnaia revoliutsiia (Opyt Turkestana),* (Moscow: Gosizdat, 1921), p. 42.

6. E. B. Bekmakhanov, *Prisoedinenie Kazakhstana k Rossii* (Moscow: Akademiia Nauk SSSR, Institut istorii, 1957), p. 168.

7. A. A. Kaufman, *K voprosu o russkoi kolonizatsii Turkestanskogo Kraia* (St. Petersburg: MZ i G. I., 1903), pp. I–VII.

8. Safarov, *loc. cit.*

9. S. D. Asfendiarov, *Natsionalno-osvoboditelnoe vosstanie 1916 g. v. Kazakhstane* (Alma-Ata–Moscow: Kazakhskoe Kraevoe izd., 1936), p. 184.

10. S. Brainin, *Amangeldy Imanov* (Alma-Alta–Moscow: Kazakhskoe Kraevoe izd., 1936), pp. 50 ff.

11. Asfendiarov, *op. cit.,* pp. 77 ff, 101–5.

Chapter 2: The Revolution

1. Safarov, *op. cit.*, pp. 50 ff.
2. The production of cotton had already fallen by half.
3. Safarov, *op. cit.*, p. 78.
4. Safarov, *op. cit.*, pp. 82–84.
5. S. B. Ginsburg, "Basmachestvo v Fergane," *Novyi Vostok* (No. 10–11, 1925), pp. 184–5.
6. A. I. Ishanov, *Sozdanie Bukharskoi Narodnoi Sovetskoi Respubliki* (Tashkent: Ak. Nauk UzSSR, 1955), pp. 61 ff.
7. K. Mukhammedberdyev, *Kommunisticheskaia partia v borbe za pobedu narodnoi revoliutsii v Khorezme* (Ashkhabad: Turk. Gosizdat, 1959), pp. 66 ff.
8. Safarov, *op. cit.*, pp. 86–87.
9. Mukhammedberdyev, *op. cit.*, pp. 80, 90–92.
10. Safarov, *op. cit.*, p. 100.
11. Mukhammedberdyev, *op. cit.*, pp. 100–49.
12. V. I. Lenin, *O Sredrei Azii i Kazakhstane,* "Zamechaniia na proekte Turkestanskoi Komissii" (Tashkent: Gosizdat UzSSR, 1960).
13. Sultan Galiev, a Tatar Communist-nationalist who disputed Stalin's theories, was arrested in 1928, kept in the Solovki concentration camp from 1929 to 1939. He disappeared in 1940.
14. Alexandre Bennigsen et Chantal Quelquejay, *Les mouvements nationaux chez les Musulmans de Russie; Le sultangalierisme au Tatarstan* (Paris-Hague: Mouton & Co., 1960), p. 138.
15. V. I. Lenin, *op. cit.*, pp. 571–72.
16. Mukhammedberdyev, *op. cit.*, pp. 154–66, 179.
17. Ishanov, *op. cit.*, p. 59.
18. *Ibid.*, pp. 71–85.
19. *Ibid.*, p. 142.

Chapter 3: The Basmachi Revolt

1. Safarov, *op. cit.*, p. 91.
2. S. B. Ginsburg, "Basmachestvo v Fergane," *Novyi Vostok,* (No. 10–11, 1925), pp. 187–91. Madamin-bek was caught during the summer of 1920 by the forces of Kur-Shirmat, turned over to another Basmachi chieftain, Khal-Hodja, and killed by the latter.
3. *Ibid.*, pp. 192–4.
4. T. Kh. Keldiev, *Razgrom Kontrrevoliutsii v Ferganskoi i Samarkandskoi oblastiakh Turkestanskoi ASSR (1918–23),* (Tashkent: Gosizdat UzSSR, 1959).

5. Ginsburg, *loc. cit.*

6. Akademiia Nauk Uzbekskoi SSR, *Istoriia sovetskogo gosudarstva i prava Uzbekistana,* Vol. I, 1917–1924 (Tashkent, 1959), p. 55.

7. T. Ryskulov, "Sovremenny Kazakhstan," *Novyi Vostok* (No. 12, 1926), p. 112.

8. Mukhammedberdyev, *op. cit.,* pp. 200–24 ff, 251–6.

9. M. Irkaev, W. Nikolaev, Ia. Sharapov, *Ocherki Istorii Sovetskogo Tadzhikistana (1917–1957),* Stalinabad: Tadzhik Gosizdat, 1957), pp. 77–79.

10. *Istoriia sovetskogo gosudarstva i prava Uzbekistana,* p. 162.

11. A. Briskin, *Strana Tadzhikov* (Moscow-Leningrad: Gosizdat, 1930), pp. 37–38.

12. A. Kh. Babakhodzhaev, *Proval aggressivnoi politiki angliiskogo imperializma v Srednei Azii 1917–1920 g.* (Tashkent: izd. Akademii Nauk UzSSR, 1955), p. 142.

13. *Vtoroi Vseuzbekskii s"ezd Sovetov . . . Stenograficheskii otchet* (Tashkent: TsIK Sovetov UzSSR, 1927), p. 131.

14. A. Listovskii, *Boevye zapiski (iz dnevnika budenovtsa),* Moscow: Ogiz Molodaia Gvardia, 1934), p. 7.

15. Vasilevskii, "Fazy basmacheskogo dvizheniia v Srednei Azii," *Novyi Vostok,* Vol. 29, 1930, p. 134.

16. Sh. Z. Urazaev, *Turkestanskaia ASSR i ee gosudarstvennopravovye osobennosti* (Tashkent: Gosizdat UzSSR, 1958), pp. 146–7.

17. M. N., "Pod znakom islama," *Novyi Vostok* (No. 4, 1923), p. 93.

18. D. Soloveichik, "Revoliutsionnaia Bukhara," *Novyi Vostok* (No. 2, 1922), p. 287.

19. Ginsburg, *op. cit.,* pp. 195–8.

20. *Istoriia sovetskogo gosudarstva i prava Uzbekistana,* pp. 74–80.

21. Ginsburg, *op. cit.,* p. 199.

22. Keldiev, *op. cit.,* p. 121.

23. Ginsburg, *op. cit.,* p. 200.

24. Anatolii Maier (ed.), *Boevye epizody Basmachestva v Fergane i Khorezme* (Moscow-Tashkent: Gosizdat, 1934), pp. 65, 73.

25. A. Briskin, *op. cit.,* pp. 44–46.

26. *Pervyi Vseuzbekskii s"ezd sovetov . . . Stenograficheskii otchet* (Tashkent: TsIK UzSSR, Feb. 1925), p. 27.

27. *Vtoroi s"ezd, op. cit.,* pp. 21, 51, 53.

28. *Pervyi s"ezd, op. cit.,* pp. 106–7.

29. *Vtoroi s"ezd, op. cit.*, p. 86.

30. Briskin, *op. cit.*, p. 60.

31. Riszard Wraga, *Sowieckie republiki srodkowo-azjatyckie* (Rome: Biblioteka Orla Bialego), 1945, p. 92.

32. T. R. Ryskulov, *Kirgizstan* (Moscow: Ogiz, Sotsegiz, 1935), p. 67.

Chapter 4: Economic Life

1. *Istoriia sovetskogo gosudarstva i prava Uzbekistana*, p. 23.

2. *Kazakhstan*, p. 129.

3. S. Dimanshtein, "Desiat let natsionalnoi politiki partii i sovvlasti," *Novyi Vostok*, No. 19 (1927), p. XVIII.

4. John D. Littlepage, *In Search of Soviet Gold* (New York: Harcourt, Brace & Co., 1938), pp. 108–9.

5. *Kazakhstan*, Introd. by Nurpeisov (Moscow: Sotsegiz, 1936), p. 150.

6. General Paul Tubert, *L'Ouzbekistan, république sovietique* (Paris: Editions du Pavillion, 1951), pp. 42–43; *Kazakhstan, op. cit.*, p. 149.

7. T. R. Rakhimbaev, *Tadzhikistan* (Moscow: Sotsegiz, 1936), p. 50; Ryskulov, *op. cit.*, p. 89; M. Belocki, *Kirgizskaia Respublika* (Moscow: Sostegiz, 1936), p. 37.

8. H. Seton-Watson, "Soviet Nationality Policy," *The Russian Review*, Vol. XV (No. 1, Jan. 1956), p. 9.

9. USSR People's Commissariat of Justice, *Anti-Soviet Bloc of Rightists and Trotskyites* (*Report of Court Proceedings*), *verbatim report* (Moscow, 1938), pp. 223–4.

10. Paul B. Henze, "The Economic Development of Central Asia to the Eve of World War II," *Journal of the Royal Central Asian Society*, Vol. XXXVII (1950), p. 47.

11. Nestor Korol, "The So-Called Virgin Lands of Kazakhstan," *Marquette University Slavic Institute Papers*, No. 14 (1962), pp. 10, 17.

12. Kari-Niiazov, *loc. cit.;* Sh. N. Ulmashbaev, *Promyshlennoe razvitie sovetskogo Uzbekistana, Istoriko-ekonomicheskii ocherk* (Tashkent: Gosizdat Uzbekskoi SSR, 1958), pp. 165, 168; Zh. Kalymbetov, *Kommunisticheskaia partiia Uzbekistana v borbe za razvitie promyshlennosti (1941–1945 gg)*, (Tashkent: Gosizdat Uzbekskoi SSR, 1958), p. 26.

13. Henry A. Wallace, *Soviet Asia Mission* (New York: Reynal & Hitchcock, 1946), p. 104.

14. *Narodnoe khoziaistvo Uzbekskoi SSR*, pp. 139–40.

15. Kalymbetov, *op. cit.*, pp. 10, 16, 81–83, 86.

16. *Narodnoe khoziaistvo Uzbekskoi SSR*, p. 32, gives the following 1945 figures: (1940 = 100) City of Tashkent—201; Regions: Tashkent—148, Namangan—49, Andizhan—80, Samarkand—76, Kaska-Darya—58, Khorezm—49, Kara-Kalpak ASSR—53.

17. Samarkand. Statisticheskoe upravienie, *Narodnoe Khoziaistvo Samarkandskoi oblasti. Statisticheskii sbornik* (Samarkand, 1958), p. 13.

18. Kalymbetov, *op. cit.*, pp. 95–96.

19. *Istoriia Kommunisticheskoi Partii Sovetskogo Soiuza* (Moscow: Gospolitizdat, 1959), p. 545.

20. Kalymbetov, *loc. cit.*

21. *Narodnoe khoziaistvo Uzbekskoi SSR*, pp. 53, 55, 56, 76, 77. Land under vegetables decreased from 38,600 hectares in 1940 to 22,600 in 1950.

22. *Pravda Vostoka*, April 29, 1943.

Chapter 5: The Settlers

1. Richard E. Pipes, "The Soviet Impact on Central Asia," *Problems of Communism*, Vol. VI, No. 2 (1957), p. 28.

2. S. S. Balzak, V. F. Vasiutin, Ya. G. Feigin, *Ekonomicheskaia geografiia SSSR* (Moscow: Akademiia Nauk SSSR, Institut Ekonomiki, 1940), Vol. I, p. 152.

3. Pipes, *loc. cit.*, p. 29.

4. The Poles had been arrested in the Western Ukraine and Byelorussia at the time of Soviet occupation in 1939–1940 and deported to Siberia as "unreliable elements." They were released after the resumption of Soviet-Polish (London) relations following the German attack on Russia.

5. Samarkand. *Kratskii spravochnik—putevoditel*, Compiled by I. I. Umniakov, *et al.* (Tashkent: Gosizdat Uzbekskoi SSR, 1956), p. 66.

6. Robert C. Tucker, "Impressions of Russia in 1958. A Trip Report" (A Rand Corp. Paper, 1958), p. 43.

7. P. Alampiev, *Soviet Kazakhstan* (Moscow: Foreign Languages Publishing House, 1958), p. 71.

8. Richard Pipes, *Moslems of Soviet Central Asia: Trends and Prospects* (Cambridge: Massachusetts Institute of Technology, Center for International Studies, 1954), p. 6.

9. Helene Carrere d'Encausse, "Réalités et limites de la presence russe en Asie Centrale," *L'Afrique et l'Asie*, No. 44 (4th trim. 1958), p. 5; H. Carrere d'Encausse et A. Bennigsen, "Pouvoir

apparent et pouvoir réel dans les républiques musulmanes de l'URSS," *Problèmes Soviétiques*, No. 1 (1958), p. 58; Hans Koch und Leo Bilas, "Slawen und Asiaten in der UdSSR," *Osteuropa*, No. 7/8 (1958), p. 425.

10. Arkhipov, *op. cit.*, p. 35.

11. Joachim Barth, "Wieviel Menschen kann Russisch-Asien ernähren?" *Osteuropa*, Vol. VI, No. 2 (1956), p. 102.

12. Edouard Sablier, "Au pays de l'Islam rouge," *Le Monde* (June 26–July 5, 1956), June 30, 1956.

13. A. Bennigsen, "The USSR and the Colonial Revolution," in *The Middle East in Transition. Studies in Contemporary History*, Walter Z. Laqueur, ed. (New York: Frederick A. Praeger, 1958), p. 410.

14. *Uzbekistan za 40 let Sovetskoi vlasti*, pp. 108–10.

15. Monteil, quoting *Izvestiia*, November 17, 1938.

16. "Bolshe vnimaniia natsionalnym kadram promyshlennosti," *Pravda Vostoka*, January 9, 1941.

17. *Ibid.*, September 24, 1946.

18. *Ibid.*, November 19, 1946.

19. Communist Party of Uzbekistan. Institut istorii partii pri TsKKP Uzbekistana, *Rezoliutsii i resheniia s"ezdov KP Uzbekistana* (Tashkent: Gosizdat UzSSR., 1957), pp. 402, 436.

20. Kalymbetov, *op. cit.*, p. 86.

21. G. G. Gimpelson, A. P. Sheliubskii, "O predposylkakh i osobennostiiakh velikoi oktiabrskoi sotsialisticheskoi revoliutsii v Srednei Azzii," *Istoriia SSSR*, No. 5 (Sept.–Oct., 1959), p. 7.

Chapter 6: Cultural Policy

1. R. Randot, "L'experience sovietique chez les peuples turcs de l'Asie Centrale," *L'Afrique et l'Asie* (December 1948), p. 8. Adoption of the Russian alphabet was considered, but rejected for fear of raising the question of attempted Russification.

2. Serge A. Zenkovsky, *Pan Turkism and Islam in Russia* (Cambridge: Harvard University Press, 1960), p. 2.

3. Walter Kolarz, *Russia and Her Colonies* (London: George Philip and Son, Ltd., 1952), p. 36.

4. N. A. Baskakov, "Razvitiie iazyka i pismennosti narodov SSSR," as quoted by S. Wurm, *Turkic Peoples of the USSR: Their historical background, their language and the development of Soviet linguistic policy* (London: Central Asian Research Center in association with St. Anthony's College, Oxford, 1954), p. 48.

5. Leonard Barnes, *Soviet Light on the Colonies* (London: Pen-

guin Books, 1944), pp. 213–15, and Hans Niedermeier, "Schriftreform und Nationalitaten in der UdSSR," *Osteuropa,* Vol. III, No. 6 (Dec. 1956), p. 416.

6. II. D. Desheriev, *Razvitie mladopismennykh narodov SSSR* (Moscow: Uchpedgiz, 1958), p. 218.

7. A. Bennigsen, "Les limites de la destalinization dans l'Islam sovietique," *L'Afrique et l'Asie,* No. 39 (1957), pp. 30–31.

8. Allworth, *The Soviet Russian Impact on Uzbek Literary Activity.* Unpublished Ph.D. dissertation, Columbia University, 1959, p. 209.

9. Wurm, *op. cit.,* pp. 45–47.

10. Desheriev, *op. cit.,* p. 224.

11. A. R. Mordinov, "O razvitii iazykov sotsialisticheskikh natsii v SSR," *Voprosy Filosofii,* No. 3 (1950), p. 92.

12. I. P. Tsamerian, "Velikaia Oktiabrskaia sotsialisticheskaia revoliutsiia i korennoe izmenenie natsionalnykh otnosheniiv SSSR," *Voprosy Filosofii,* No. 5 (1957), pp. 61, 65. See also Elliott R. Goodman, "The Soviet Design for a World Language," *The Russian Review,* Vol. XV, No. 1 (Jan. 1956), for a description of Soviet views on the Russian language as the world language of the future.

13. Mary Matossian, "Two Marxist Approaches to Nationalism," *American Slavic and East European Review,* Vol. XVI (December 1957), p. 499.

14. Jindrich Kucera, "Soviet Nationality Policy: The Linguistic Controversy," *Problems of Communism,* Vol. III, No. 2 (1954), p. 24.

15. A. Bennigsen, "Les peuples musulmans de l'URSS et les Soviets," 2nd part, "Le conflit culturel," *L'Afrique et l'Asie,* No. 21 (1953), pp. 17–23.

16. *Ibid.,* based on *Antologiia Tadzhikskoi poezii* (Moscow, 1951); Gafurov, *Istoriia Tadzhikskogo naroda,* Vol. I (Moscow, 1949); *Antologiia Uzbekskoi poezii* (Moscow, 1950); *BSE,* 2nd ed., Vol. I, p. 467; V. V. Struve in *Sovetskoe vostokoznanie,* Vol. V (1948), pp. 5–35.

17. Allworth, *op. cit.,* pp. 9, 101–2, 204.

18. "Islam," *BSE,* 1st ed., Vol. 29, and *Pravda Vostoka,* June 29, 1950.

19. Monteil, "Essai," p. 65, quoting *Soviet War News* (May 16, 1942), and Monteil, "Supplement à l'essai sur l'Islam en URSS," *Revue des Études Islamiques,* Vol. XIII (Paris, 1953), p. 8, quoting *Mir Islama* (No. XI, 1913), pp. 269–271.

20. Monteil, "Essai," p. 46, and verbal accounts by Polish refugees. From 1947 on, atheistic propaganda was again given free sway. See also Raymond K. Kent, "Soviet Muslims, The Arab World and the Myth of Synthesis," *Journal of International Affairs*, Vol. XIII, No. 2 (1959), p. 143.

21. *Ibid.*, p. 17 (quoted from *Dawn*, July 28, 1952).

22. Jan Dubicki, *Elements of Disloyalty in Turkmenistan* (Russian text), (New York: Research Program on the USSR, 1954), pp. 16–17.

23. Caroe (Sir Olaf Kirkpatrick), *Soviet Empire. The Turcs of Central Asia and Stalinism* (London: Macmillan and Co., 1953), p. 240.

24. Konstantin F. Shteppa, "The Lesser Evil Formula," in *Rewriting Russian History. Soviet Interpretations of Russia's Past*, ed. by C. E. Black, published for the Research Program on the USSR (New York: Frederick A. Praeger, 1956), p. 110.

25. A. Bennigsen, "Les limites de la destalinization," *L'Afrique et l'Asie*, No. 39 (1957), p. 32.

26. See *ibid.* and Paul B. Henze, "The Shamil Problem," in *The Middle East in Transition. Studies in Contemporary History*, ed. by Walter Z. Laqueur (New York: Frederick A. Praeger, 1958), pp. 417 ff., for a detailed description of the Shamil question.

27. See Bennigsen, "Les peuples musulmans de l'URSS," *op. cit.*, No. 22, p. 27 ff., for a detailed account of the Manas affair.

28. *Ibid.*, pp. 23–24.

29. Compiled by Monteil, "Essai sur l'Islam en URSS," pp. 113–115, from *Voprosy Istorii* (No. 9, 1952); *Vestnik Akademii Nauk* (June 1952); *Literaturnaia Gazeta* (February 14 and June 8, 1952); *Bakinskii Rabochii* (July 18, 1950). The latter stated, "The Azerbaijani people (during the Shamil revolt) waited with impatience for the arrival of the Russian soldier-liberators."

30. Bennigsen, "Les peuples musulmans de l'URSS," *op. cit.*, No. 23, p. 19 ff.

31. Kolarz, *op. cit.*, pp. 268–69.

32. Wayne S. Vusinich, "Moslems of the Soviet Union," *Current History*, Vol. XXIV, No. 137 (January 1953), pp. 9–11.

33. A. Iakubovskii, "Serioznoe issledovanie po istorii tadzhikskogo noroda," *Kommunist*, No. 1 (Jan. 1953), p. 103.

34. Hans Kohn, *Pan-Slavism: Its History and Ideology* (Notre Dame: University of Notre Dame Press, 1953), p. 250.

35. H. Carrere d'Encausse, "La destalinization dans l'Islam sovietique," *L'Afrique et l'Asie*, No. 37 (1957), pp. 32–36.

36. Bennigsen, "Les limites de la destalinization," *op. cit.*, No. 39, p. 35.

37. For the prerevolutionary situation see: Serge A. Zenkovsky, "Kulturkampf in Pre-Revolutionary Central Asia," *The American Slavic and East European Review*, Vol. XIV, No. 1 (February 1955), p. 20, and Massalskii, *op. cit.*, pp. 336–339. For the post-revolutionary development see: *BSE*, 1st ed., Vol. LV; *ibid.*, 2nd ed., Vol. XII, p. 435; Central Asian Review, Vol. III, No. 1 (1955), p. 70.

38. *Ibid.*

39. Compare *BSE*, 1st ed., Vol. LV, p. 640; *Central Asian Review*, Vol. III, No. 1 (1955), p. 70; *U. N. Statistical Yearbook, 1954*, Table 372, p. 532 (Iran); *Statistical Abstract of the United States* (Washington, D. C., 1954), pp. 128, 131, 137 (North Carolina and South Carolina).

40. According to *BSE*, 2nd ed., Vol. XII, p. 435, in per cents of the population nine years of age and older: Uzbekistan—67.8 per cent; Turkmenistan—67.2 per cent; Tajikistan—71.7 per cent; Kirgizstan—70 per cent.

41. Dubicki, *op. cit.*, p. 37.

42. Lt. Col. G. E. Wheeler, "Cultural Developments in Soviet Central Asia," *Journal of the Royal Central Asian Society*, Vol. XLI (1954), p. 182.

43. Monteil, "Essai sur l'Islam en URSS," p. 94.

44. *Pravda Vostoka*, March 23, 1945.

45. *20-letie Sredne-Aziatskogo Universiteta* (Tashkent, 1940), pp. 20–21, and Monteil, *Les musulmans sovietiques* (Paris: Editions du Seril, 1957), p. 96.

46. *Narodnoe khoziaistvo USSR v 1961 godu*, pp. 691, 693, 700.

47. Tubert, *op. cit.*, pp. 82–83.

48. Monteil, *Les musulmans sovietiques*, pp. 74, 114, according to Mrs. Mukhitdinova, head of the Work Among Women section of the Uzbek Central Committee's secretariat.

49. *Rezoliutsii i resheniia s"ezdov KP Uzbekistana*, p. 364. The Tenth Party Congress in Uzbekistan was forced to acknowledge that many Uzbek girls were dropping out of school.

50. Monteil, *Les musulmans sovietiques*, p. 112. *Pravda Vostoka* (October 6, 1955), states that between 1947 and 1955 only 172 high school diplomas were awarded to native girls in the city of Samarkand (i.e., an average of about 29 a year).

51. B. Nikitin, "Problème national et évolution technique en Asie sovietique," *L'Afrique et l'Asie*, No. 31 (1955), p. 21.

52. Pipes, "The Soviet Impact on Central Asia," p. 32.

53. Eric Downton, "Soviet Central Asia," *Journal of the Royal Central Asian Society*, Vol. XLII (1955), p. 131.

Chapter 7: The Cadres, the Elite and the People

1. Joseph Stalin, *On the National Question* (London: Lawrence and Wishart, 1942), p. 29.

2. T. H. Rigby, "Social Orientation and Distribution of Membership in the Communist Party of the Soviet Union," *The American Slavic and East European Review*, Vol. XVI (October 1957), p. 275, presumes the four principles mentioned to be the guiding force of the Communist Party.

3. Monteil, "Essai sur l'Islam en l'URSS," pp. 57–58.

4. *Anti-Soviet Bloc, op. cit.*, pp. 213, 239, 746.

5. Dr. A. Godkepe, "The National Policy of Moscow. Ezhov's Purges in Turkestan," *Turkeli*, No. 3–4, (March–April, 1952), pp. 7–8.

6. "Partiinaia organizatsiia i avtoritet direktora," *Pravda Vostoka*, February 6, 1941.

7. *Ibid.*, June 3, 1941.

8. As compiled from *Pravda Vostoka*, 1941–1946.

9. "Sobranie partiinogo aktiva v Samarkande," *ibid.*, March 19, 1941.

10. Herbert S. Dinerstein, "The Sovietization of Uzbekistan. The First Generation," in *Russian Thought and Politics*, ed. by H. McLean, M. E. Malia, O. Fisher, Vol. IV of *Harvard Slavic Studies* (Cambridge, Mass.: Harvard University Press, 1957), p. 512.

11. Patrick Sergeant, *Another Road to Samarkand* (London: Hodder & Stoughton, 1955), p. 110.

12. Seton-Watson, *op. cit.*, p. 8.

13. Rigby, *op. cit.*, p. 290.

14. *Ibid.*, p. 277.

15. Caroe, *op. cit.*, pp. 246–253, and Dubicki, *op. cit.*, pp. 44–47, as related by eyewitnesses.

16. *Pravda Vostoka*, October 5, 1946.

17. Rigby, *op. cit.*, p. 281.

18. *Pravda Vostoka*, August 24, 1946.

19. *Ibid.*, editorial, Sept. 15, 1957.

20. In the Kashka-Darya region only 33 out of 703 collective

farms had Party organizations (*Pravda Vostoka,* October 10, 1943).

21. *Ibid.,* October 5, 1946. The Sixteenth Plenum of the Tashkent Party Committee; *Ibid.,* August 17, 1943, mentions a conference of the collective-farm elite in the Samarkand region attended by 1,500 members of the rural elite.

22. *Ibid.,* August 20, 1942.

23. *Ibid.,* May 12, 1941.

24. *Ibid.,* editorial, August 24, 1946.

25. *Ibid.,* October 5, 1946. The Sixteenth Plenum of the Tashkent Regional Party Committee.

26. M. Rywkin, *The Soviet Nationalities Policy and the Communist Party Structure in Uzbekistan, 1941–46.* Unpublished Ph.D. dissertation, Columbia University, 1960, Appendix, Table 25.

27. *Ibid.,* Tables 23 and 24.

28. S. P. Trapeznikov, "Istoricheskaia rol MTS v sozdanii i ukreplenii kolkhoznogo stroia," *Vosprosy Istorii KPSS,* No. 2 (1958), p. 52. Recently MTS machinery was sold to collective farms, and MTS themselves were eliminated.

29. See, for example, "V prokurature UzSSR," *Pravda Vostoka,* December 17, 1943.

30. M. Dubinskii, "V Ak-Darye pokrovitelstvuiut zhulikam," *ibid.,* June 24, 1944.

31. *Ibid.,* July 28, 1943.

32. M. Dubinskii, "Nikuda ne godnyi stil raboty Samarkandskogo Oblzo," *ibid.,* May 14, 1944.

33. "It was necessary last year to replace about 10 collective farm chairmen recommended [read: "appointed"] by the District Party Committee," admits *Pravda Vostoka,* January 29, 1941.

34. S. Galitskii, "Nepravilnyi podkhod k vospitaniiu kolkhoznykh kadrov," *ibid.,* May 24, 1944.

35. *Ibid.,* May 14, 1944, quotes two examples, one in Bukhara, another in the Samarkand region.

36. Joseph Stalin, *Marxism and the National Question. Selected Writings and Speeches* (New York: International Publishers, 1942), pp. 193–94.

37. *Ibid.,* p. 160.

38. *Pravda,* November 2, 1946.

39. As quoted by C. Barghorn, *Soviet Russian Nationalism* (New York: Oxford University Press, 1956), p. 69.

40. See *Komsomolskaia Pravda,* November 15, 1952.

41. *Pravda Vostoka*, October 5, 1946, stated that half of the new Party members in some of the districts of the Tashkent region recruited in 1945 were illiterate or semiliterate.

42. *Ibid.*, editorial, October 23, 1943.

43. John Parker, "Impressions of the Soviet Middle East," *Journal of the Royal Central Asian Society*, Vol. XXXIII (1946), describes how he was entertained by a local Moslem Party secretary who, in ordering an artist to appear, clapped his hands as the Emir must have done in prerevolutionary days.

44. Dinerstein, *op. cit.*, pp. 509–13.

45. Parker, *op. cit.*, p. 349, cites that a home built for a local Party secretary had separate quarters for women. Walter McKenzie Pinter, "Initial Problems in the Soviet Economic Development of Central Asia," *Journal of the Royal Central Asian Society*, Vol. XL (1953), p. 295, states the same in respect to newly built housing for native workers.

46. Andre Pierre, "Religion in Soviet Land," *Problems of Communism*, Vol. IV, No. 3 (May–June 1955), p. 26. See also *Rezoliutsii i resheniia s"ezdov kommunisticheskoi partii Uzbekistana*, p. 470, concerning the condemnation by the Thirteenth Uzbek Party Congress (1956) of the feudal attitude toward women on the part of many native Communists.

47. Patrick Sergeant, *op. cit.*, p. 130.

48. *Ibid.*, p. 121.

49. A. Bennigsen, "The Moslem Intelligentsia in the USSR," *Soviet Survey*, No. 28 (April–June 1959), pp. 9–10.

50. Dubicki, *op. cit.*, pp. 43–47, and according to Polish refugees' accounts.

51. Caroe, *op. cit.*, pp. 246–53. Safarov, *op. cit.*, pp. 80, 83, 91.

52. Baymirza Hayit, *Turkestan im XX Jahrhundert* (Darmstadt: C. W. Leske Verlag, 1956), pp. 344–46.

Chapter 8: The Party Apparatus

1. Rywkin, *op. cit.*, Appendix, Table 2.

2. Rywkin, *op. cit.*, Tables 1 and 26. Same in 1961 (see *Pravda Vostoka*, Feb. 5, 1962).

3. A. Bennigsen, "The Moslem Intelligentsia in the USSR," *op. cit.*, p. 8.

4. Compiled by Bennigsen from *Kazakhstanskaia Pravda* (Jan.

27, 1956); *Sovetskaia Kirgiziia* (Aug. 27, 1956); *Turkmenskaia Iskra* (Jan. 27, 1956); *Kommunist Tadzhikistana* (Jan. 31, 1956) and *Pravda Vostoka* (Jan. 29, 1956).

5. Koch and Bilas, *op. cit.*, p. 429.

6. Mark Alexander (W. Z. Laqueur), "Tensions in Soviet Central Asia," *The Twentieth Century* (September 1951), p. 193. See also Downton, *op. cit.*, p. 131.

7. S. S. Studenikin, V. A. Vlasov, I. I. Evtikhiev, *Sovetskoe administrativnoe pravo* (Moscow: Gosizdat Iuridicheskoi literatury, 1950), pp. 6–8.

8. Julian Towster, "Recent Trends and Strategies in Soviet Federalism," *The Political Quarterly,* Vol. XXIII, No. 2 (1952), p. 165.

9. See John N. Hazard, "Soviet Public Administration and Federalism," *The Political Quarterly,* Vol. XX (1949), pp. 7–8, and *Konstitutsiia Soiuza SSR i Konstitutsiia Soiuznykh Respublik* (Moscow: Iuridizdat, 1938).

10. Rywkin, *loc. cit.*, Tables 5, 6, and 7.

11. H. Carrere d'Encausse, "La politique musulmane des Soviets dans une republique plurinationale le Daghestan," *L'Afrique et l'Asie* (No. 34, 1956), p. 37, considers this a standard policy in both Union and autonomous republics.

12. Monteil, *Les musulmans sovietiques,* p. 54.

13. Rywkin, *loc. cit.*

14. W. W. Kulski, *The Soviet Regime. Communism in Practice* (Syracuse: Syracuse University Press, 1956), p. 194, confirms the total lack of activity on the part of the Ministers of Foreign Affairs and Defense of the Union Republics (the United Nations delegations of Ukraine and Byelorussia excepted).

15. *Pravda Vostoka,* December 27, 1944; October 20 and March 11, 1945.

16. Rywkin, *loc. cit.*, Appendix, Table 7.

17. *Pravda Vostoka,* Sept. 28, 1943.

18. Institute for the Study of the USSR (Munich). *Biographic Directory of the USSR* (New York: Scarecrow Press, Inc., 1958), p. 66.

19. M. H. Yarcek, "Moscow's Administration in Turkestan," *Milli Turkisan,* No. 6 (11), 83 (Dec. 1952–Jan. 1953), pp. 34–36.

20. Ten out of 24 in Kazakhstan; 16 out of 20 in Kirgizstan and 13 out of 19 in Turkmenistan (Bennigsen, "The Moslem Intelligentsia in the USSR," p. 7).

21. Rywkin, *op. cit.*, Appendix, Table 28.

22. Bennigsen, *loc. cit.*, also Carrere d'Encausse and Bennigsen, *op. cit.*, p. 62.

23. Louis Nemzer, "The Kremlin's Professional Staff," *American Political Science Review*, XLIV (March, 1950), p. 65.

24. Milovan Djilas, "The New Class," *An Analysis of the Communist System* (New York: F. A. Praeger, 1956), p. 60.

25. Merle Fainsod, *How Russia is Ruled* (Cambridge: Harvard University Press, 1956), p. 192.

26. ————, *Smolensk Under Soviet Rule* (Cambridge: Harvard University Press, 1958), p. 67.

27. *Pravda Vostoka*, June 20, 1941.

28. See Rywkin, *loc. cit.*, Appendix, Tables 8–17, 27.

29. Bulaq Baschi, "The Country Which Has Not Yet Capitulated," *Milli Turkistan*, No. 6 (April–May 1953), p. 29, gives the following percentage of Russians among the Party secretaries in Soviet Central Asia in the early 1950's: first secretaries of Regional Party Committees—30 per cent; second secretaries—80 per cent; first secretaries of District Party Committees—20 per cent; second secretaries—90 per cent; heads of Regional Party Committee departments—90 per cent. The first four figures resemble my 1940 figures. The last one, however, seems strongly exaggerated by both 1940 and 1950 standards.

30. Fainsod, *How Russia is Ruled*, p. 192.

31. *Pravda Vostoka* (January 27, 1946). See also Appendix, Table 12.

32. Derek R. Scott, *Russian Political Institutions* (New York: Rinehart & Company, Inc., 1957), p. 165.

33. H. Carrere d'Encausse, *loc. cit.*, "La politique musulmane des Soviets . . ."

34. H. Seton-Watson, *op. cit.*, p. 8.

35. Kalymbetov, *op. cit.*, p. 12.

36. *Pravda Vostoka*, September 14, 1946.

37. Kalymbetov, *loc. cit.*

38. Fainsod, *How Russia is Ruled*, p. 520.

39. Monteil, *Les musulmans sovietiques*, pp. 55–56.

40. *Pravda Vostoka*, June 12, 1941.

41. Carrere d'Encausse and Bennigsen, *op. cit.*, p. 64; and Monteil, *Les musulmans sovietiques*, pp. 55–56.

42. Fainsod, *Smolensk Under Soviet Rule*, p. 68.

43. *Pravda Vostoka*, December 8, 1944, and March 5, 1946.

44. *Ibid.*, July 31, 1946.

45. See "School of Marxist-Leninist preparation of Soviet cadres" (*ibid.*, December 1, 1946) and the Decree of the Central Committee of the All-Union Communist Party (bolsheviks) of November 14, 1938, concerning the organization of the Party propaganda in connection with the publication of the *Short Course of the History of the Communist Party of the Soviet Union.*

46. Fainsod, *Smolensk Under Soviet Rule*, p. 70.

47. The Twentieth Plenum of the Samarkand Regional Party Committee (August 1946), which was entirely devoted to "Measures to be taken in order to strengthen the struggle against the perversion of the collective-farm status and the plundering of collective-farm property" (by the farmers themselves), shows, however, that the Regional Party Committee had also to cope with other problems in agriculture (*Pravda Vostoka*, August 17, 1946).

48. *Ibid.*, April 2, 1943.

49. *Ibid.*, October 1, 1943, and M. Dubinskii, "Plody samodovolstviia . . . ," *ibid.*, August 31, 1943.

50. U. Iusupov, "O nedostatkakh i oshibkakh v rabote Andizhanskogo Obkoma," *ibid.*, September 28, 1944.

51. *Ibid.*, September 29 and October 17, 1944, and *ibid.*, May 22, 1945.

52. "Stil raboty selsko-khoziaistvennogo otdela Samarkandskogo Obkoma Partii," *ibid.*, April 10, 1945.

53. *Ibid.*, May 17, 1944.

54. *Ibid.*, October 17, 1944, and March 5, 1946.

55. *Ibid.*, August 17, 1946, and September 19, 1942.

56. *Ibid.*, February, 1941; July 6, August 17 and December 31, 1943; March 5, October 1, 1946; etc.

57. *Ibid.*, July 10, 1942.

58. *Ibid.*, November 24, 1946.

59. Kalymbetov, *op. cit.*, p. 13.

60. "Gruboe narushenie vnutrepartiinoi distsipliny," *Pravda Vostoka*, August 20, 1946.

61. Rywkin, *op. cit.*, Appendix, Tables 19 and 22.

62. *Ibid.*, Table 18.

63. *Pravda Vostoka*, May 31, 1944.

64. N. Subach, "Kolkhoznyi ustav-nerushimyi zakon," *ibid.*, May 26, 1944.

65. S. Galitskii, "Nepravilnyi podkhod k vospitaniiu kolkhoznykh kadrov," *ibid.*, May 24, 1944.

66. *Ibid.*, June 24, 1944, and Plenum of the Samarkand Re-

gional Party Committee, *ibid.*, August 17, 1946. For example, in the Kara-Darya district, see *ibid.*, December 5, 1944.

67. N. Dubinskii, "Chem zaniat sekratar Raikoma," *ibid.*, July 25, 1943; M. Dzhalilova, "Slova i dela Pskentskikh rukovoditelei," *ibid.*, July 23, 1943, and "V Bulungure zanimaiutsia mitingami," *ibid.*, April 1, 1945.

68. Article by M. Dubinskii, *ibid.*, June 20, 1945.

69. *Ibid.*, August 6, 1944.

70. *Ibid.*, November 23, 1946.

71. *Ibid.*, September 27, 1946.

72. *Ibid.*

73. "Sekretar Raikoma v roli zazhimshchika kritiki," *Pravda*, November 18, 1946.

74. *Pravda Vostoka*, January 4 and 29, 1941.

75. *Ibid.*, March 14, 1941.

76. Fainsod, *Smolensk Under Soviet Rule*, pp. 114–115.

77. *Pravda Vostoka*, April 11, 1941.

78. *Ibid.*, July 31, 1943.

79. Ecker, *op. cit.*, pp. 53–54.

80. A. Barsukov (instructor of the Organization-Instruction Department of the Central Committee of the C. P. [b] Uz.), "Otvetstvennost za rekomendatsii," *Pravda Vostoka*, January 30, 1941. *Ibid.*, July 21, 1946; November 15, 1944; August 21, 1946.

81. S. Galitskii, "V storone ot politicheskoi raboty," *ibid.*, October 13, 1944, and K. Nurmatov, "V Koshrabadskom raione zapushchena partinno-massovaia rabota," *ibid.*, August 13, 1944.

82. *Ibid.*, October 5, 1946, and U. Valiev, "Tam prenebregaiut organizatsionno-partiinoi rabotoi," *ibid.*, October 10, 1943.

Chapter 9: Conclusion

1. Except for a number of Turkestani defectors who fought on the German side during World War II.

2. Albert Cobban, *National Self-Determination* (Chicago: University of Chicago Press, 1947), pp. 107–108.

3. *Voprosy Istorii* (December, 1950), as quoted by Solomon M. Schwarz, "Revising the History of Russian Colonialism," *Foreign Affairs*, Vol. XXX, No. 3 (April, 1952), p. 488.

4. *Pravda Vostoka*, May 4 and February 23, 1955; *Kommunist Tadzhikistana* and *Kazakhstanskaia Pravda*, both of May 4, 1955. A Russian, A. Luchinskii, was then in command of the Turkestan Military District.

5. Rywkin, *op. cit.*, Appendix, Tables 1 and 5.

6. According to Monteil, "Supplement . . . ," p. 19: Gubin in Kazakhstan, Volodin in Kirgizstan, Baskolov in Uzbekistan, Galkin in Turkmenistan, Vishnevskii in Tajikistan. Same Gubin in Kazakhstan (*Kazakhstanskaia Pravda,* April 12, 1955), Tereshchenko in Kirgizstan (*Sovetskaia Kirgiziia,* April 6, 1955), Byzov in Uzbekistan (*Pravda Vostoka,* March 29, 1955), Vaskin in Turkmenistan (*Turkmenskaia Iskra,* March 20, 1955), Kochevoi in Tajikistan (*Kommunist Tadzhikistana,* April 1, 1955).

7. John A. Armstrong, *The Soviet Bureaucratic Elite. A Case Study of the Ukrainian Apparatus* (New York: Frederick A. Praeger, 1959), pp. 111–13.

8. *Ibid.,* pp. 120–21.

9. B. G. Gafurov, "Stroitelstvo kommunizma i natsionalnyi vopros," in *Voprosy stroitelstava kommunizma v SSSR. Materialy nauchoi sessii otdelenii obshchestvennykh nauk Akademii Nauk SSSR* (Moscow: Akademiia Nauk SSSR, 1959), pp. 96–97.

10. See, for example, Charles W. Hostler, "The Turks and Soviet Central Asia," *The Middle East Journal,* Vol. XII, No. 3 (Summer 1958), p. 268; Bennigsen, "The Moslem Intelligentsia in the USSR," p. 10, and many others.

11. Walter Z. Laqueur, "Sultan Galiev's Ghost," *The New Leader* (February 3, 1958), pp. 10–11.

12. ———, "The Shifting Line in Soviet Orientology," *Problems of Communism,* Vol. V, No. 2 (March–April 1956), p. 20.

13. N. A. Smirnov, *Ocherki po zucheniiu Islama v SSSR* (Moscow: Akademiia Nauk SSSR, 1954), p. 270.

14. *The New York Times,* May 23, 1958, p. 3.

15. Lieut. Col. Geoffrey Wheeler, "Colonialism and the USSR," *The Political Quarterly,* Vol. XXIX (1958), pp. 221–22.

16. Fitzroy Maclean, *Back to Bokhara* (London: Jonathan Cape, 1959), p. 99.

17. Sh. Rashidov, "Naveki vmeste s russkim narodom," *Kommunist,* No. 10 (July, 1959), pp. 51–52.

SELECTED ENGLISH
LANGUAGE BIBLIOGRAPHY

Selected English Language Bibliography

Bennigsen, A. and Quelquejay, C. *The Evolution of the Muslim Nationalities of the USSR and Their Linguistic Problems.* London: 1961.

Caroe (Sir Olaf Kirkpatrick). *Soviet Empire. The Turcs of Central Asia and Stalinism.* London: Macmillan & Co., 1953.

Holdsworth, Mary. *Turkestan in the Nineteenth Century.* Oxford: Central Asian Research Center, 1959.

Johelson, W. *Peoples of Asiatic Russia.* New York: American Museum of Natural History, 1928.

Kolarz, Walter. *Russia and Her Colonies.* London: George Philip & Son, Ltd., 1952.

Park, Alexander G. *Bolshevism in Turkestan, 1917–1927.* New York: Columbia University Press, 1957.

Pierce, Richard A. *Russian Central Asia, 1867–1917; a study in colonial rule.* Berkeley: University of California Press, 1960.

Pipes, Richard. *The Formation of the Soviet Union. Communism and Nationalism (1917–1923).* Cambridge: Harvard University Press, 1954.

————. *Moslems of Soviet Central Asia: Trends and Prospects.* Cambridge: Massachusetts Institute of Technology, Center for International Studies, 1954.

Stahl, Kathleen M. *British and Soviet Colonial Systems.* New York: Frederick A. Praeger, 1951.

Wheeler, Geoffrey. *Racial Problems in Soviet Muslim Asia.* London: Oxford University Press, 1960.

Wurm, Stefan. *Turkic Peoples of the USSR: Their Historical Background, Their Language and the Development of Soviet Linguistic Policy.* London: Central Asian Research Center and St. Anthony's College (Oxford), Soviet Affairs Group, 1954.

Zenkovsky, Serge. *Pan Turkism and Islam in Russia.* Cambridge: Harvard University Press, 1960.

In addition, a basic French book is to be recommended:

Monteil, Vincent. *Les musulmans sovietiques.* Paris: Editions du Seuil, 1957.

INDEX

Index